JAMES SIENA

NEW PAINTINGS AND GOUACHES

JAMES SIENA

NOVEMBER 18, 2005–JANUARY 28, 2006

PACEWILDENSTEIN

534 WEST 25TH STREET NEW YORK NY 10001

THE REALITY OF ABSTRACTION[1]

by John Yau

> It follows that to change modes is to change the world.
> –Wallace Stevens

> I don't make marks. I make moves.
> –James Siena

In an early painting, *Untitled Yellow Black*, 1991, James Siena gave himself a very simple but personally challenging procedure to enact in enamel on a smooth metal surface. While his choice of industrial materials suggests that he wanted his painting to be akin to a sign, which is to say a durable public thing, his procedure, which melds finely tuned attention and direct action, lifted the work into a realm of rapturous structure. This is one reason why viewers (and I am certainly one of them) want to look at Siena's paintings again and again. Not because we can finally figure the procedure out, which is sometimes possible and sometimes not and in any case beside the point, but because the paintings give both mind and body a deeply satisfying pleasure, which is to say that they both invite and resist understanding. It is in their resistance that we recognize that these works have nothing to do with transparency and received meaning, that what they embody is a tightly constructed visual mystery. At the same time, in addition to Siena's paintings, drawings, and prints being remarkably self-contained, they are also extraordinarily open. They invite endless inquiry because they do not propose to have the answer. In achieving this, Siena defines a philosophical position that is all too rare in a world riddled with moralizing discourse. He is neither didactic nor sweepingly declarative.

In his description of the rule governing the making of *Untitled Yellow Black*, Siena wrote:

Endless line containing black.
Line made up of acute angles.
No line may cross each other.[2]

In an exchange with the author, he wrote that he "just follows the little voices in [his] head."[3] I would suggest that Siena not only listens to these voices when he is painting, but it is this inwardness that has led him to a territory all his own.

Because *Untitled Yellow Black* is a plane in which two acutely angled, lightning-like lines (one yellow and one black) are tightly interlocked, each jagged line beckons us to isolate and follow it, to initiate an act of attentiveness that we are unlikely to complete. The discrepancy between what the painter has done, which is devote himself to, as well as be responsible for, every inch of the painting, and what our eyes end up doing, which is stop looking, throws us back on ourselves, leaving us with a question—how carefully have we ever examined what is around us? The question is at once troubling and necessary, particularly when we realize that *Untitled Yellow Black* urges us to rise out of our torpor, and does so without being either didactic or authoritarian.

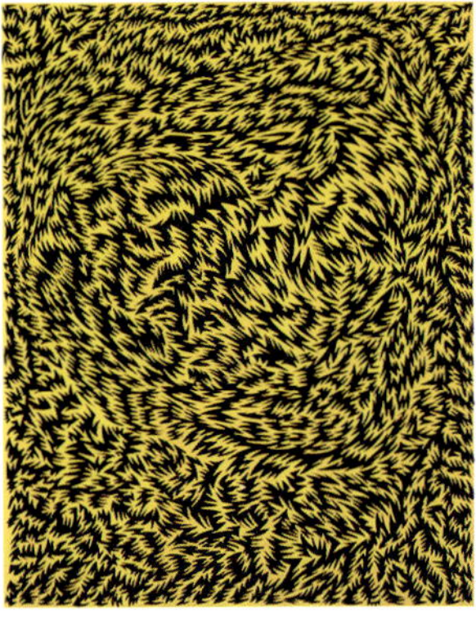

Untitled Yellow Black, 1991
enamel on aluminum, 19 1/4 x 15 1/8"

Untitled Yellow Black suggests pattern without ever settling into an overall, easily comprehensible design, which has become even truer of Siena's recent work. Even when we convince ourselves that we can see one of the artist's paintings all at once, the physically changing line, and the myriad edges against edges, tug at our eyes, cause us to zero in and scrutinize, pore over, like a possessed lover. And, as any possessed lover is apt to tell you, all that looking is constantly rewarded.

However often one of the lines echoes another, there is nothing mechanical in the paintings. Not in the least bit finicky or precious, Siena's line–and it is his and no one else's–both exerts pressure on what is contiguous to it, and is defined by the invisible stress put on it by its neighbor. It's as if the painting's plane is a force field animating everything within it. Relaxed and activated, completely at ease as well as acutely attuned to the particularities of its circumstances, each line also insists on its own primacy. The tautness between the one and the many, the single line and the multitude is one of the deep pleasures of Siena's paintings. It's as if they all took Ralph Waldo Emerson's essay "Self-Reliance" as their credo. They contribute their presence to a non-hierarchical structure (or democracy) without losing their individuality.

The loopy structural rigor of *Untitled Yellow Black* demands an equally intense response on the part of the viewer. One of the distinguishing features of this intensity is that it is both visual and physical, and, because of the scale of the painting, it occurs both at a distance and close up. For all the control that takes place within the borders of Siena's paintings, they don't privilege one vantage point over another. As in ballroom dancing, we have to keep adjusting our relationship to them, have always to be, as they say, on our toes.

During the nearly fifteen years since Siena finished *Untitled Yellow Black*, he has given himself increasingly challenging procedures, or what he calls "algorithms," to enact. I suspect that each challenge the artist meets only provokes him to defy himself further, and that his project has never been about finding a style, which finally is a mode of both consumption and production, but about sustaining an open-ended inquiry. It is like a high-stakes poker game in which there is only one player, and neither bluster nor bluffs are possible.

In maintaining this trajectory throughout the 90s and now halfway through the first decade of the 21st century, something more than complexity has steadily entered into Siena's paintings. I think the visual affinities between Siena's work and computer software, as well as its evocation of fractal models that address subatomic reality and the existence of "dark matter," is a good indication of how contemporary his work feels to us. While a number of writers have commented on the artist's relationship to pattern painting and to the algorithms found in computer software programs, all of which are insightful but somewhat incomplete readings, I would suggest that Siena's roots are far more diverse, and ultimately, whatever the sources, they all pass through Abstract Expressionism. Relying on a small brush and enamel paint, he shows no fear about embracing our often dizzying understanding of reality's components.

A recurring argument advances the view that Abstract Expressionism culminated in Pollock's poured paintings (c. 1947-51), which are said to mark both a rupture and the beginning of painting's demise. They are seen as a dividing line in history, and they represent a closed and perfect achievement that precludes anything else being done in its aftermath. In Pollock's work, as a number of influential commentators have formulated, paint became paint, and the two- dimensional surface was reified with such purity that painting was said to have arrived at its essence, which is pure abstraction. According to this line of thinking, Pollock's project was essentially complete before he died. Thus, since his death in 1956, a number of theorists have defined the ideal artist to be the one who claims to have made the last painting or, more radically, rejected painting all together in favor of a more contemporary medium.

Siena is one of a small handful of current practitioners who openly and unabashedly dispute this judgment by facing it head on. For one thing, he has inverted Pollock's project so effortlessly that his work amounts to a succinct but loving criticism of the former's groundbreaking achievement, as well as of Frank Stella's no-nonsense formalism, which is to say that his work provokes us to rethink the way we have read these two artists' work. Siena has replaced Pollock's expansive, outward movement with a rigorous inward movement, as well as transformed Stella's opticality and hard-edged lines and shapes into sensually vivid oscillations arising from a matter-of-fact hand drawn line. The connection Siena has made between drawing and line is different from what Pollock accomplished when he freed paint from the burden of being descriptive. In Siena's line one sees that he has freed it from the burden of being just paint. At the same time, he has quietly and persistently worked against the heroic scale we associate with both Pollock and Stella.[4] History, we might remind ourselves, is constantly being contested and rewritten. This isn't Siena's intention, of course. Rather, it is the natural byproduct of his work.

Contrary to what some have persuasively claimed, the history of painting did not end with Pollock and Andy Warhol. However attenuated and unlikely, history still continues, both carried on and transformed, I would argue, by iconoclasts and isolato who believe, as I am convinced Pollock did, in a continuum and are not in the least nostalgic for the past.[5] In fact, once you to begin to tease out both the affinities and differences between Siena's paintings and those of Pollock and Stella, the depth and breadth of his accomplishment, not to mention the very real mind- and eye-bending pleasure his work embodies, become all the more remarkable a thing to consider, particularly in these dark and troubling times.

The first and most obvious differences to consider are methodology and scale. As everyone by now knows, Pollock developed a unique practice. He dripped paint from a stick or brush onto a bolt of unsized canvas that had been laid flat on the studio floor. The direction of the flow was the result of his body's movement rather than his hand. The explosive swirls and dynamic skeins of paint push against, as well as extend past, the painting's containing edges. Pollock's process is additive; he can't erase or take away marks he has already made. There is an unpredictable expansiveness to Pollock's work that Stella and Warhol domesticated by leveling it out and restructuring it into a static grid that implied that what lay beyond its border was the same as what lay within.

Seemingly without effort, and certainly with breathtaking economy, Siena reverses the expansiveness of Pollock and Stella, which are different, as well as conveys his understanding that reality is constantly changing field. He applies enamel paint with a brush to an aluminum surface that lies flat. Many of the paintings seem to move inward, the larger structure echoed by smaller and smaller ones. This is about the kind of looking that is never satisfied. At the same time, and in this he parallels Pollock but differs from early Stella, what is inside his painting is not what is outside. Thus, his paintings are self-contained, but they acknowledge that the world beyond their edges, however similar, is also continuously different. For all the attention he pays to his surfaces, his paintings are never about the surface. Through his relentless iterations of the surface, he bends, ruptures, morphs, and activates the plane into a pulsing, often teeming thing. In addition, many of Siena's recent paintings and drawings register their own increasing compression; they detail the artist's attempt to discover exactly how much visual information they can possibly contain without being overwhelmed by their details.

In *one, one...* (2005; p. 11), Siena begins on the painting's left side with two thin abutting lines running from top to bottom, the outer one dark brown and the inner one mustard yellow. Abutting this full-length yellow line are two slightly thicker lines, one gray-white and the other dark brown. By the seventh row over, the vertical line has shifted its orientation and reads horizontally. The sequence is one of steadily increasing compression, of the line becoming thinner and thinner, as the right side of the line always shifts in color as it splits into two lines. In contrast to Stella, who famously said, "What you see is what you see," Siena aligns himself with Willem de Kooning, who characterized painting as a "slipping glimpse." This is not simply a stylistic difference; it is a philosophical one whose implications have yet to be fully explored. For one thing, it suggests that seeing is always partial and incomplete, that one must work to see more.

In *Recursive Lighthouse* (2004; p. 33), Siena articulates a tripartite structure made up of three vertical and horizontal black lines whose ends curve in opposite directions, like an extremely attenuated S. Within each rectangular and triangular space enclosed by the lattice of horizontal and vertical lines, he repeats the configuration but uses less than three vertical or horizontal lines. He does this three times, and then within the small areas that are left he paints concentric lines that echo their outer configuration.

In reading the painting from overall structural configuration to smaller and smaller structures, and finally to line within line, one moves from the macro to micro. At the same time, Siena's lines activate the surface, forming images without ever losing their own identity. The curves at the top and bottom, as well as those along the side, slowly bend the paint plane on all sides, pushing the middle of the painting forward. We go from looking at a surface to seeing a thing. At the same time, the figure (or lighthouse) is recursive; the figure becomes the ground and vice versa. Thus, looking means our eyes keep moving as well as shifting focus. Siena's painting does not let us retreat into our bodies and become passive.

In *Coffered Divided Sagging Grid* (2005; p. 53), Siena devises an electric blue grid, whose structural lines he further defines by two dark blue lines. He divides the irregular rectangles and triangles by diagonal lines connecting opposite corners. This causes the painting to structurally shift from rectangles to triangles. This shift from one thing to another is a current running throughout all of Siena's work. No matter how much repetition occurs within a work, there is always a constant shifting, a continuous change. Thus, within the rectangles and triangles, the artist draws increasingly smaller, echoing lines. Using the electric blue grid as key, the color progression goes from blue to orange to red, and then starts all over again. It is worth noting that Siena essentially uses three colors within a grid painting that generates interior rectangles. There is a connection between the kind of structure the artist establishes and the number of colors he uses. One senses that Siena has certain parameters in mind from the outset, and that they apply to both the structure and the color.

Siena's grid doesn't come across as an idealization, but as a thing. Sometimes it sags under the weight of its paint and reality, two actualities we seldom think of as meshing together. In this sense, without ever trying to replicate or abstract it, his abstract paintings are true to reality. For as we all know, repetition is life, both its seriousness and its exhilaration. This I think is Siena's indisputable achievement. He has taken up where Pollock left off. He has done so by eschewing the heroic, and by deciding to be responsible for every inch of his paintings. There is a parable in this that is so obvious it doesn't need telling.

Endnotes

1. Robert Hobbs, *James Siena: 1991-2001*, exh. cat. (New York: Gorney Bravin + Lee; Los Angeles: Daniel Weinberg Gallery, 2001). The statement was made by James Siena, p. 8.
2. Ibid. Hobbs asked Siena to discuss the procedures he followed. At the end of the catalogue are notes Siena sent Hobbs, all written after the paintings were completed.
3. Email to the author, October 5, 2005.
4. Perhaps it is time we began to trace the very rich, largely overlooked history of those who rejected heroic scale in favor of an intimate scale.
5. On my list of exhibitions that have yet to happen, one is devoted to exploring the affinities and differences running through the work of Piet Mondrian, Burgoyne Diller, Alfred Jensen, Charles Seliger, Eva Hesse, Bruce Conner, James Siena, Thomas Nozkowski, Daniel Zeller, and Simon Frost. Among other things, the accompanying catalogue essay would mention Jasper Johns' hatch paintings (1972-81). The title of the exhibition is "Parameters."

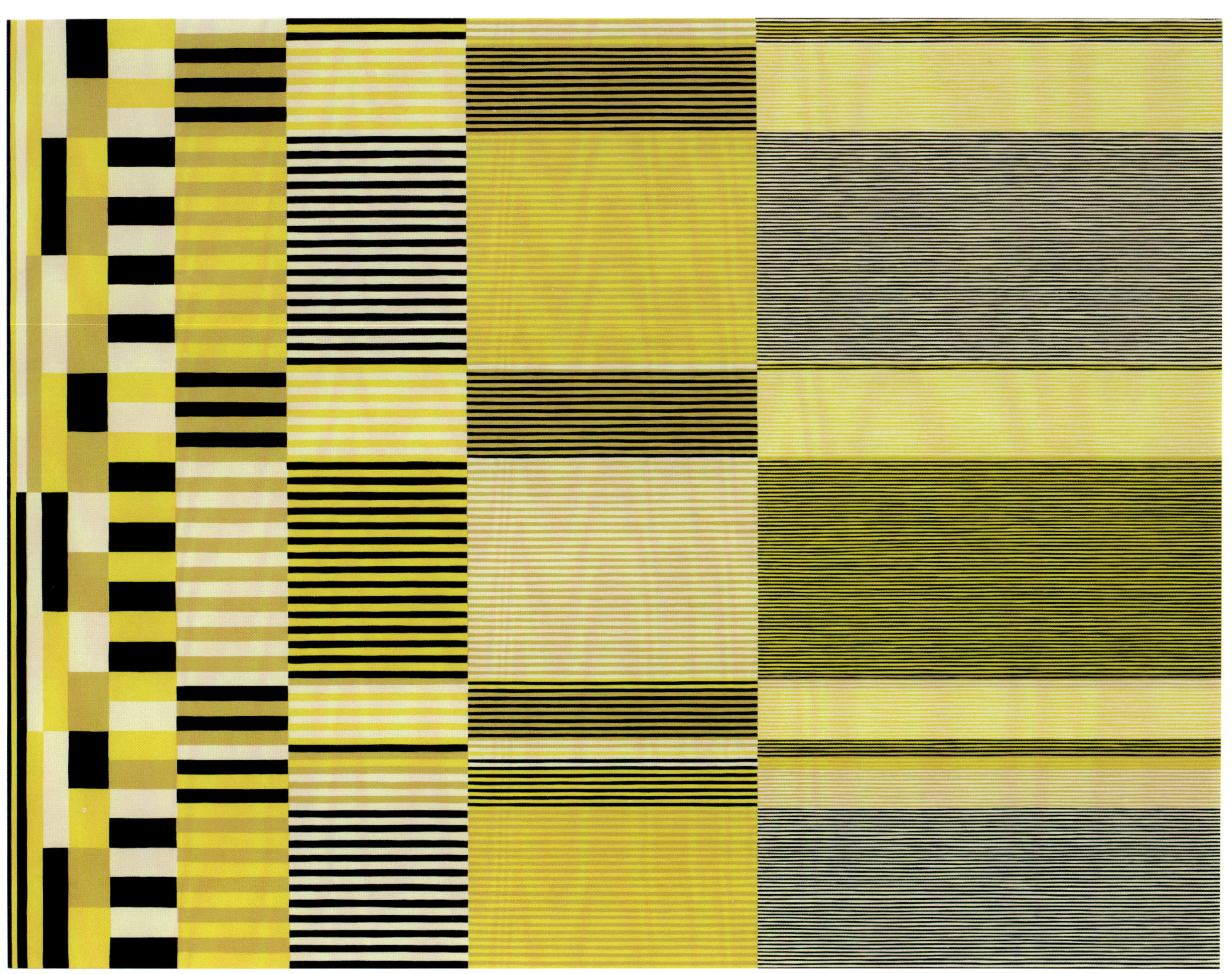

one, one... 2005, enamel on aluminum, 22 3/4 x 29"

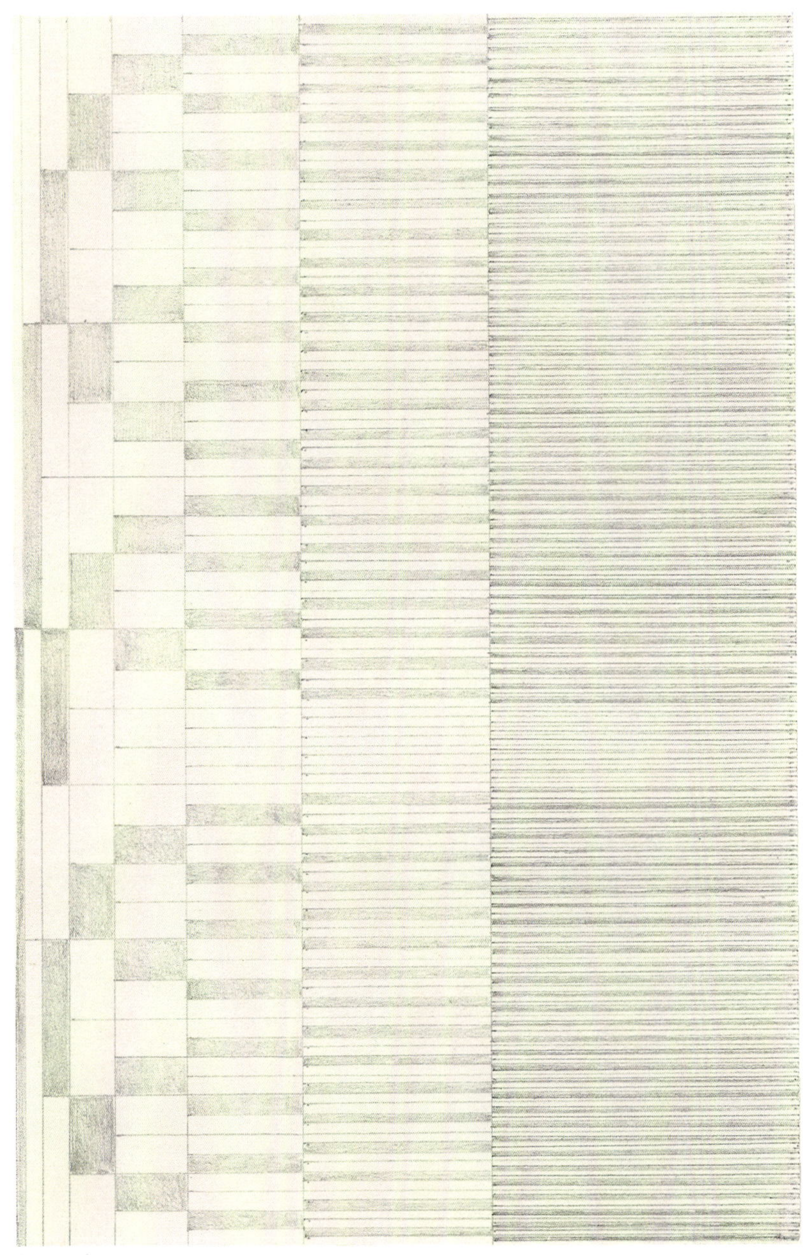

Incomplete Fibonacci Modular 2004, graphite on paper, 8 1/2 x 5 1/2"

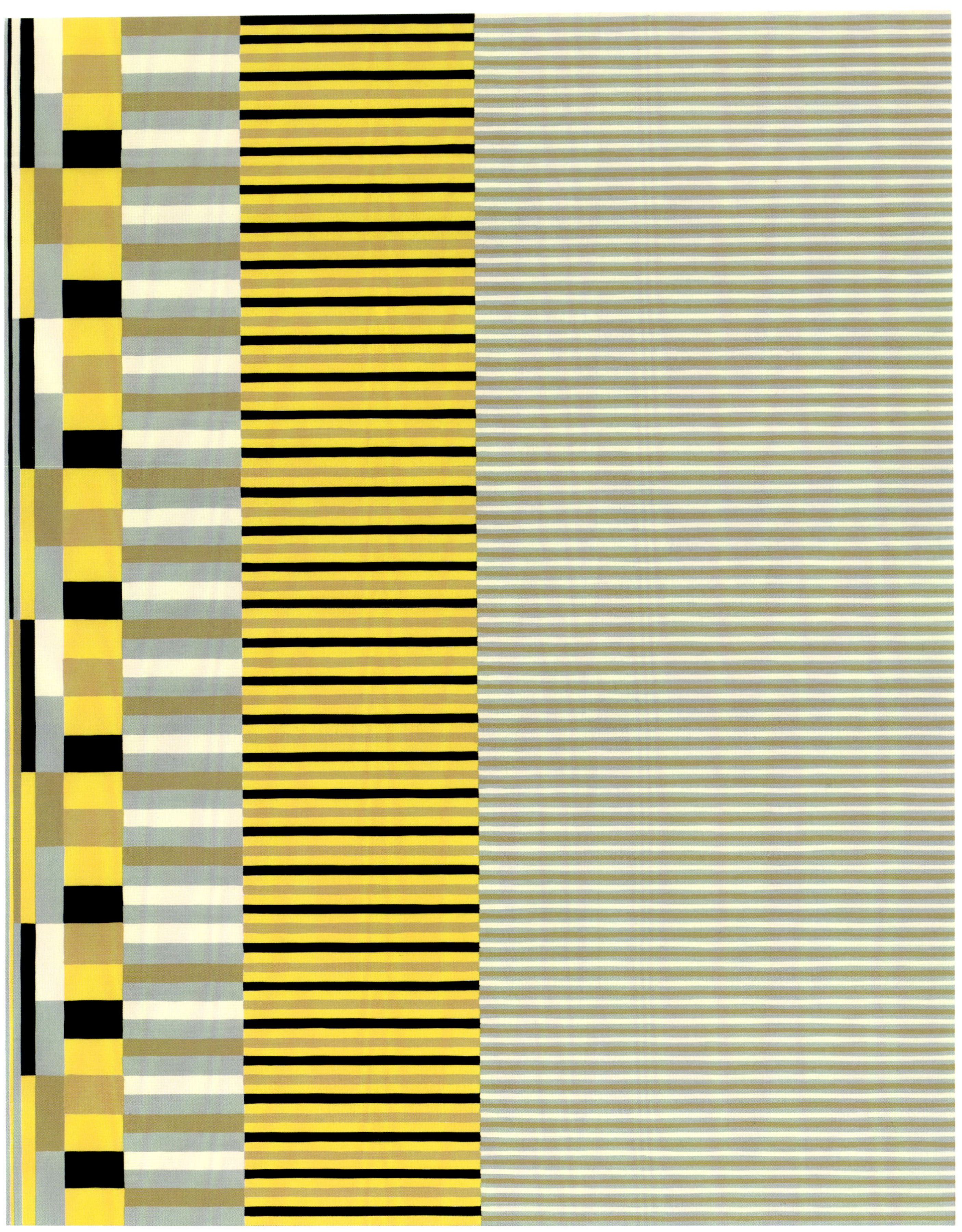

1-256, Column Doubling 2004, enamel on aluminum, 19 1/4 x 15 1/8"

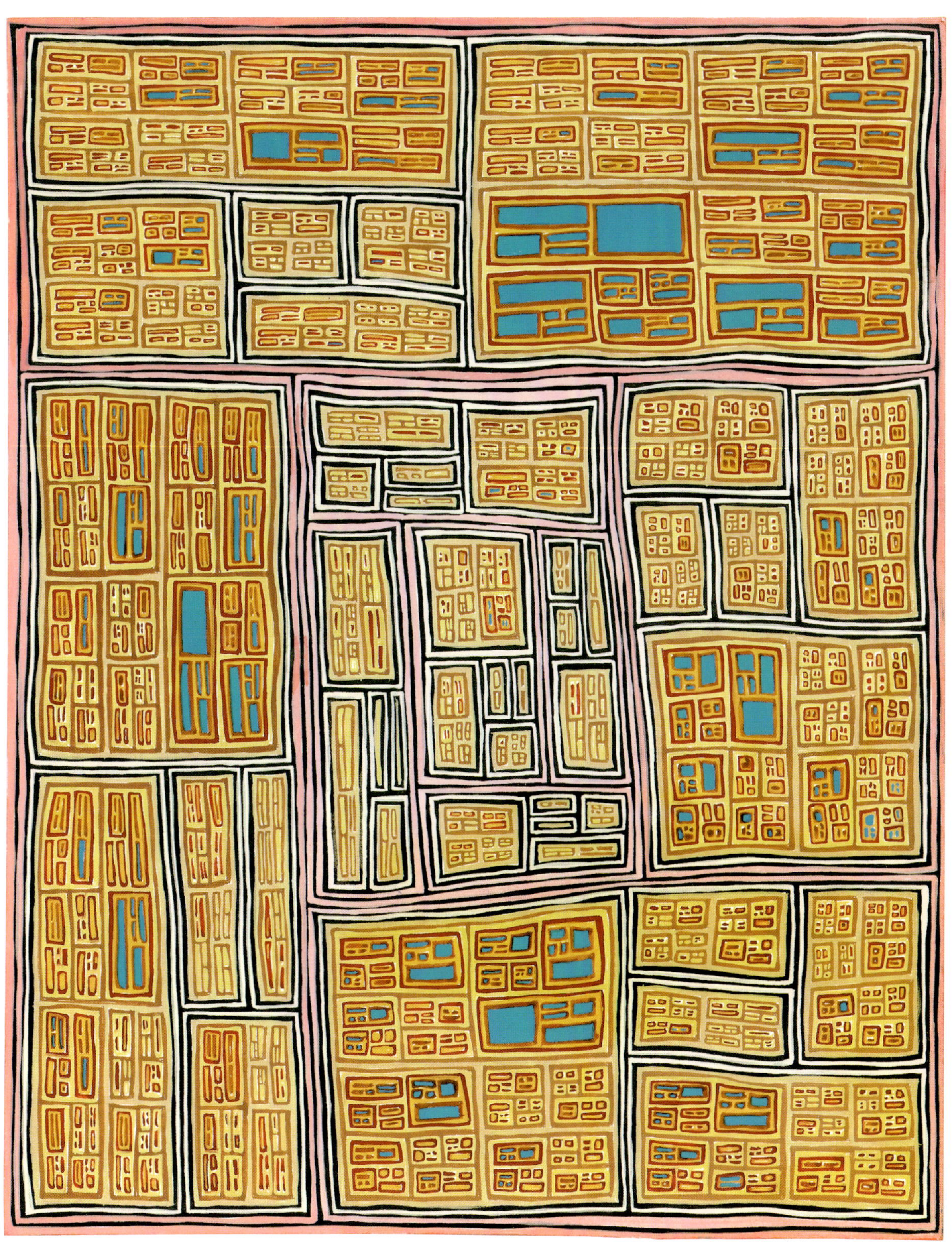

Eight Line Way (Pink) 2004–2005, gouache on paper, 11 x 8 1/2"

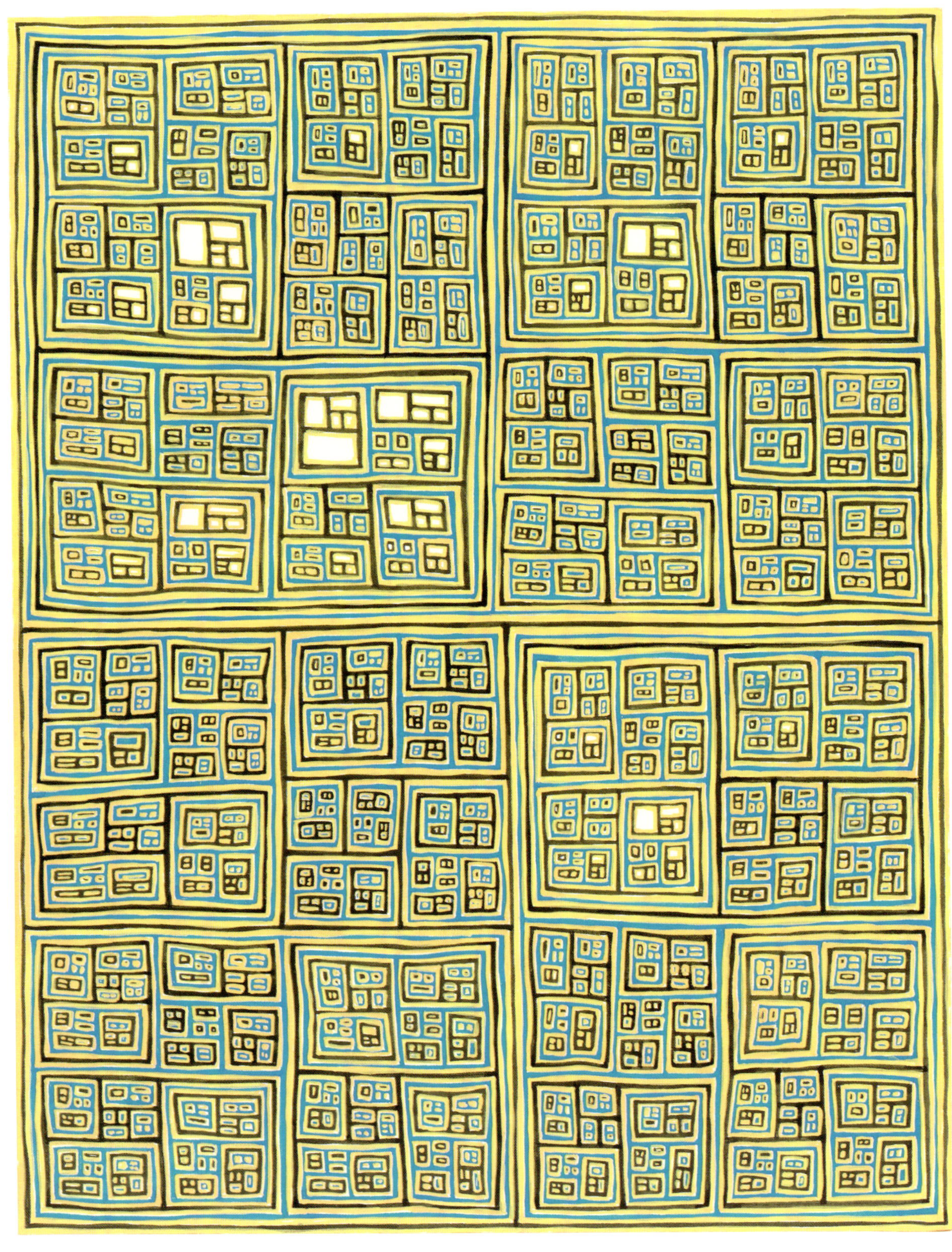

Global Key Variation 2004, gouache on paper, 11 x 8 1/2"

Multi-Colored Nesting Unknots 2004, gouache on paper, 11 x 8 1/2"

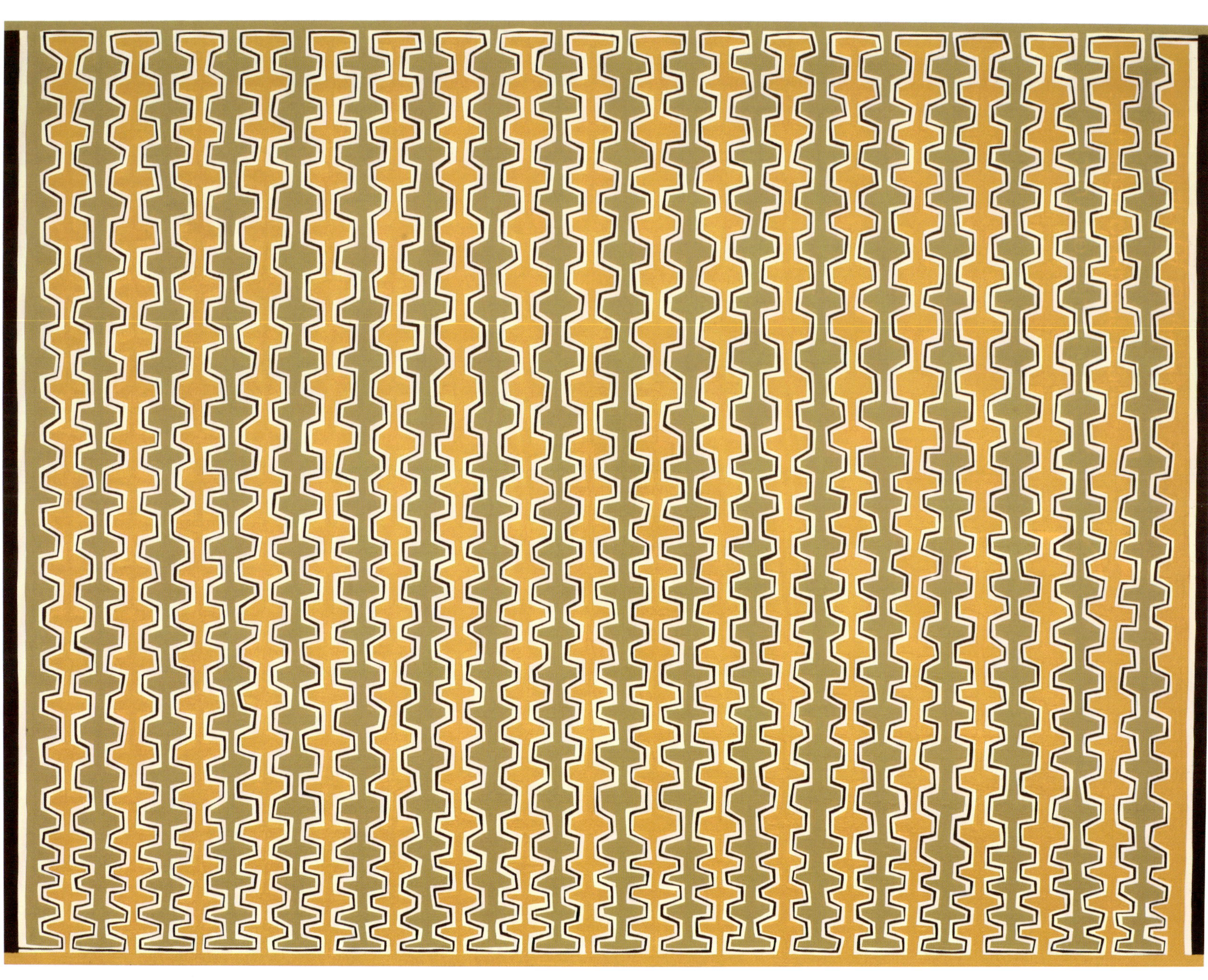

Recursive Combs, Boustrophedonic 2004, enamel on aluminum, 22 3/4 x 29 1/8"

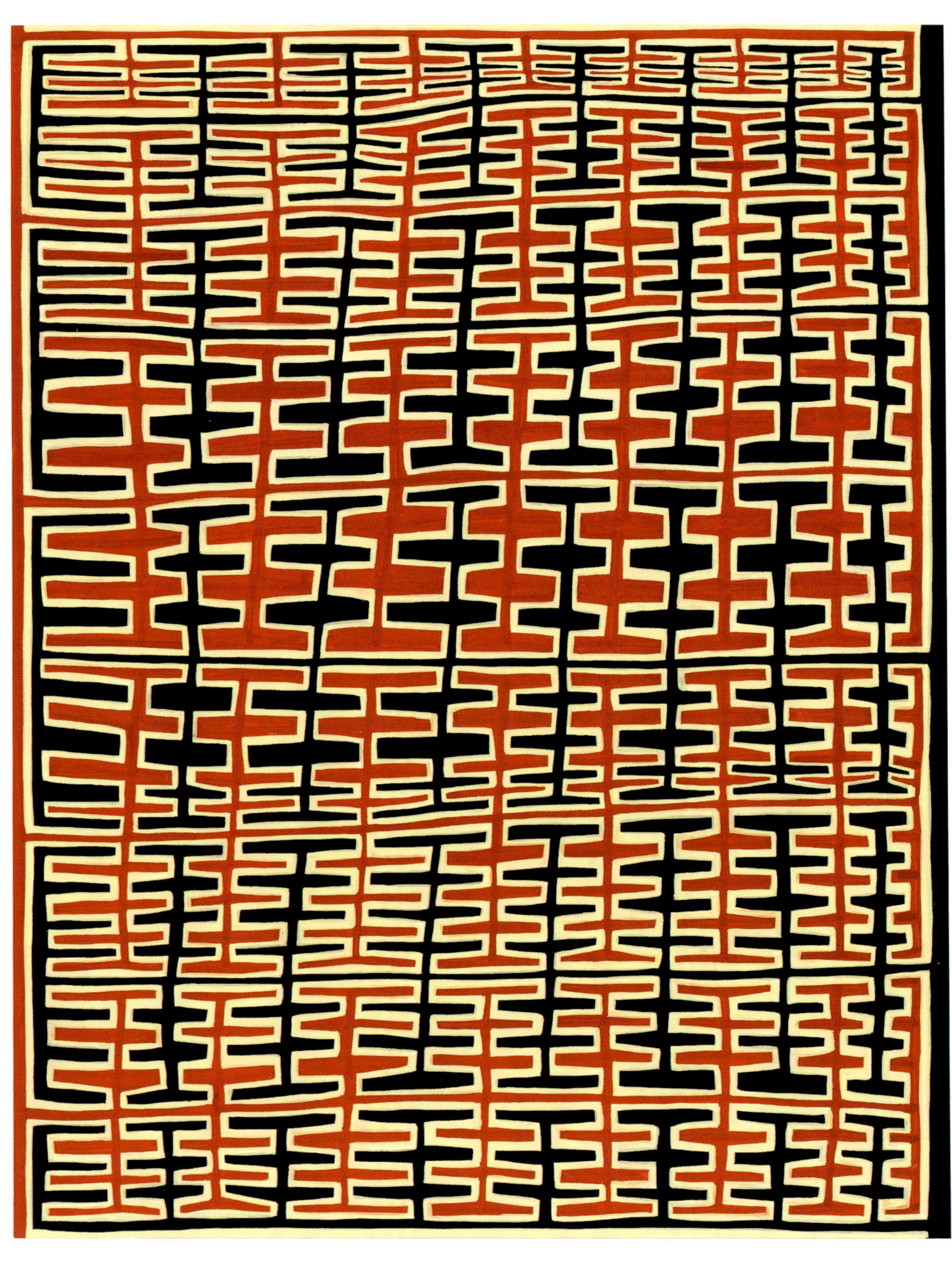

Double Recursive Combs (Red and Black) 2004–2005, gouache on paper, 11 x 8 1/2"

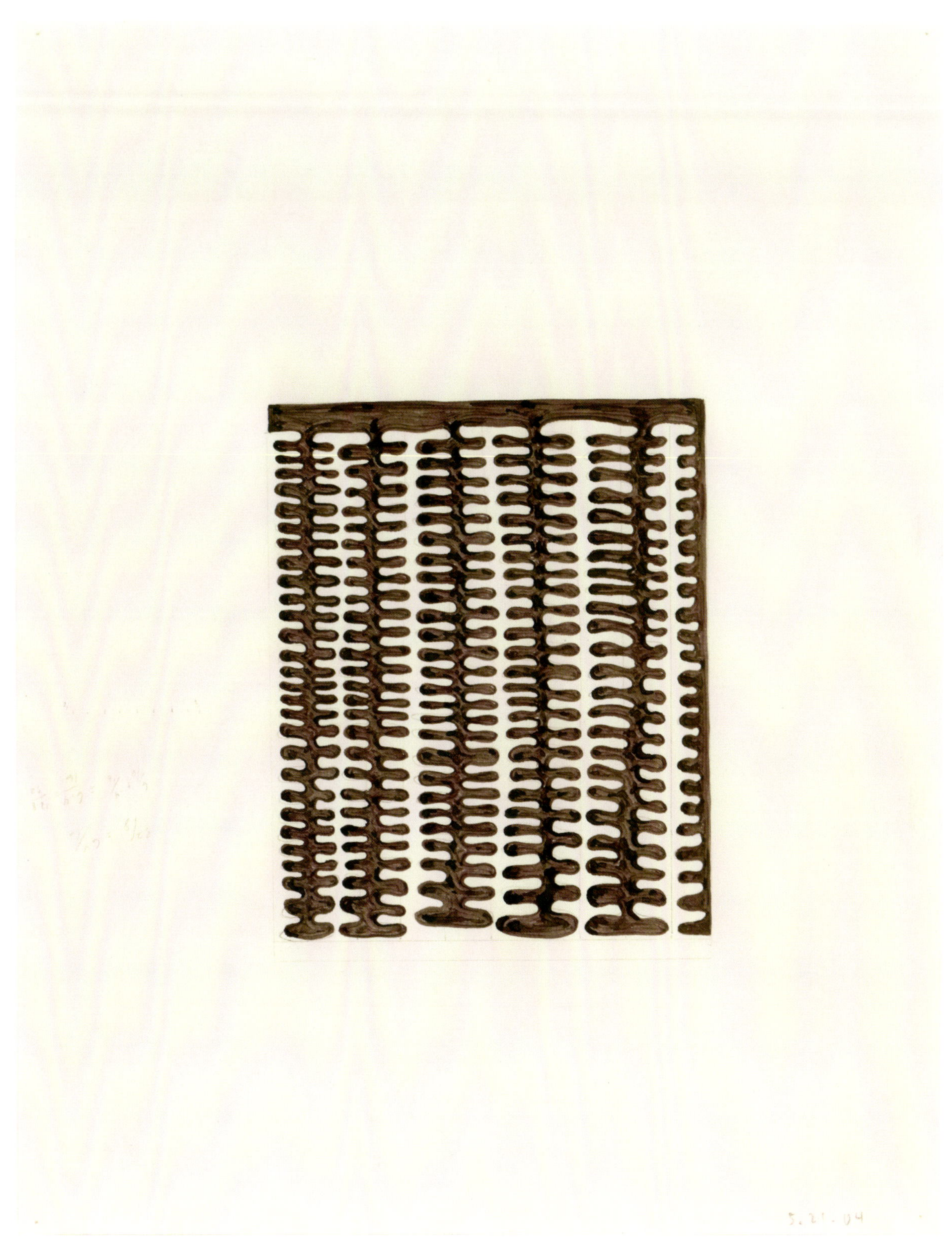

Floppy Recursive Combs 2004, ink on paper, 11 x 8 1/2"

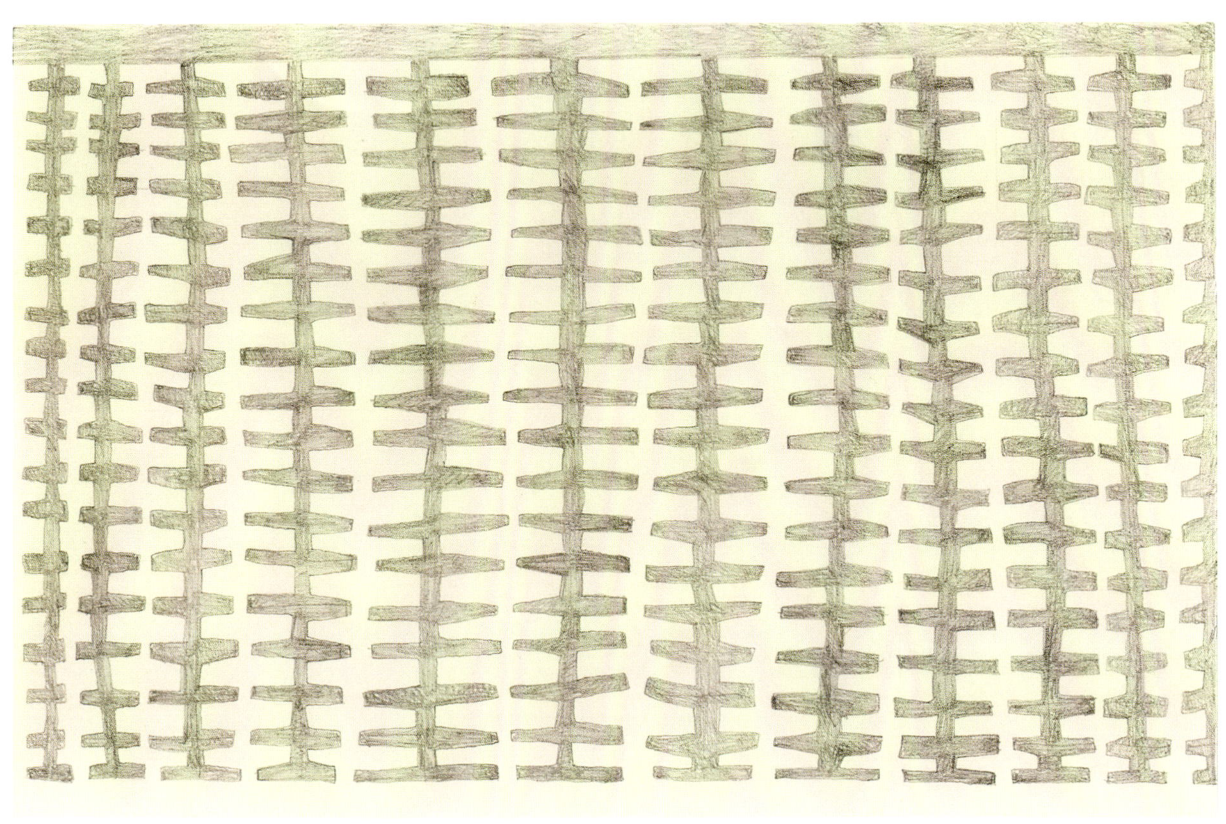

Recursive Comb (Spaceless) 2004, graphite on paper, 5 1/2 x 8 1/2"

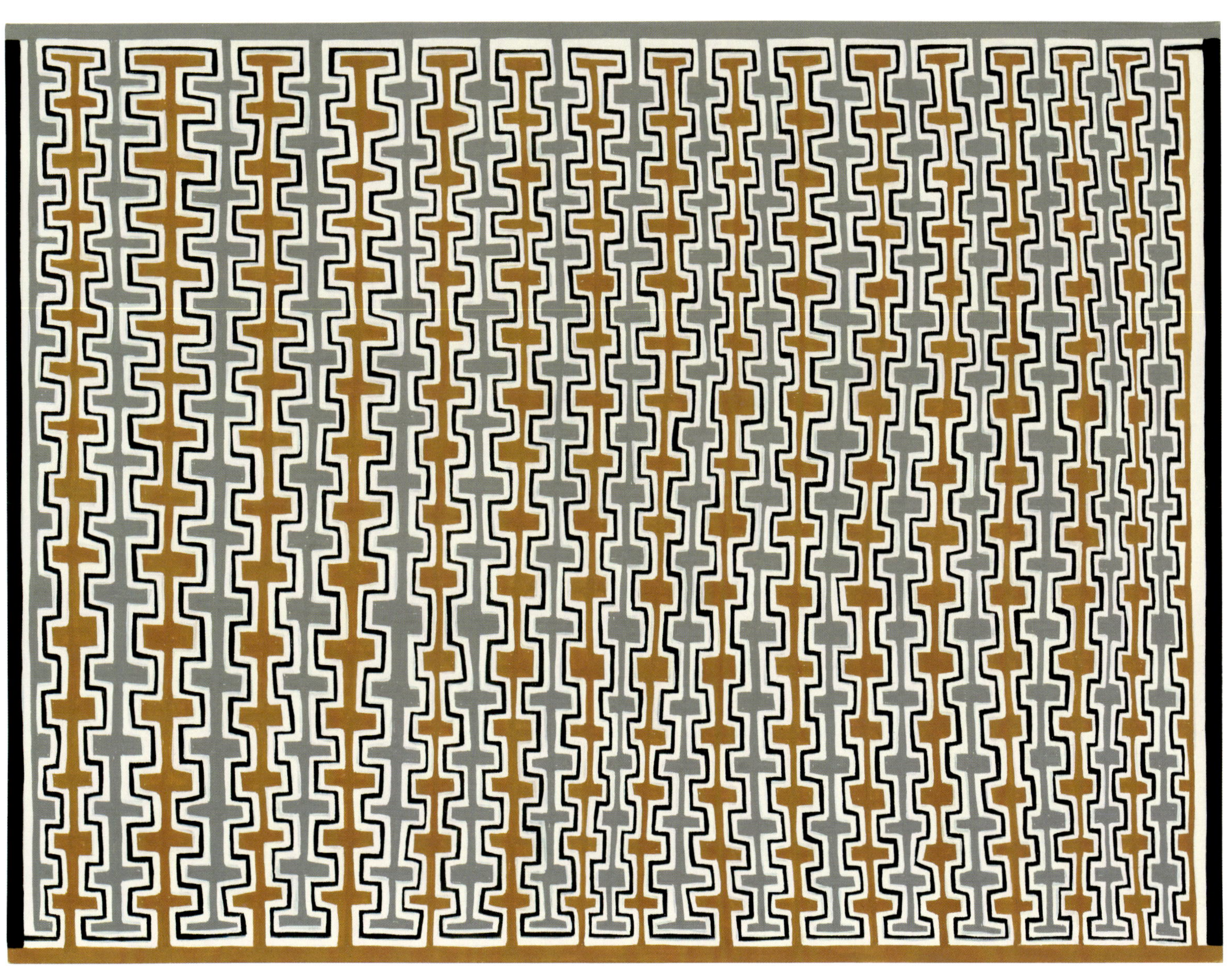

Boustrophedonic Recursive Combs 2004, gouache on paper, 8 1/2 x 11"

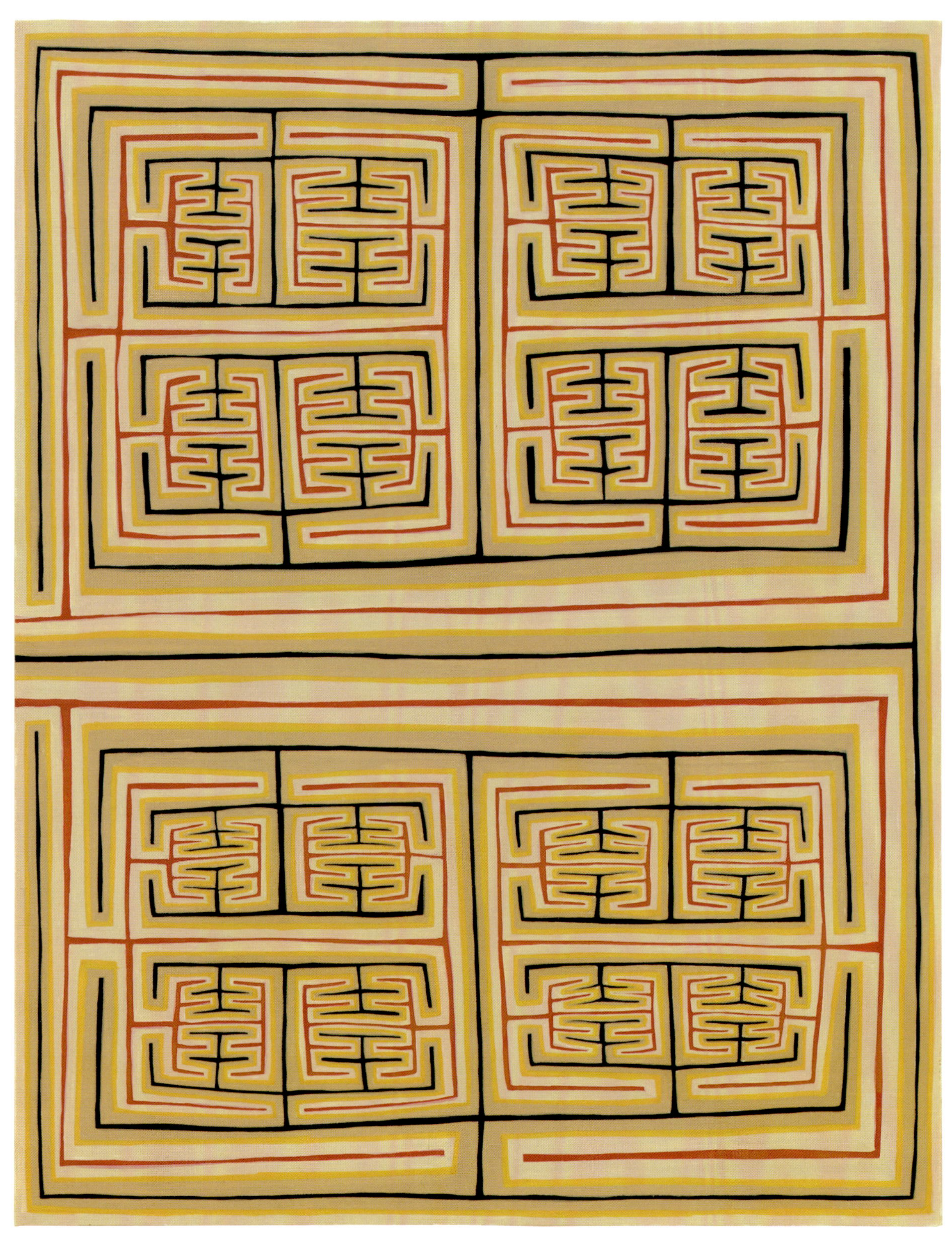

Left and Right Sides of the Walk 2005, gouache on paper, 11 x 8 1/2"

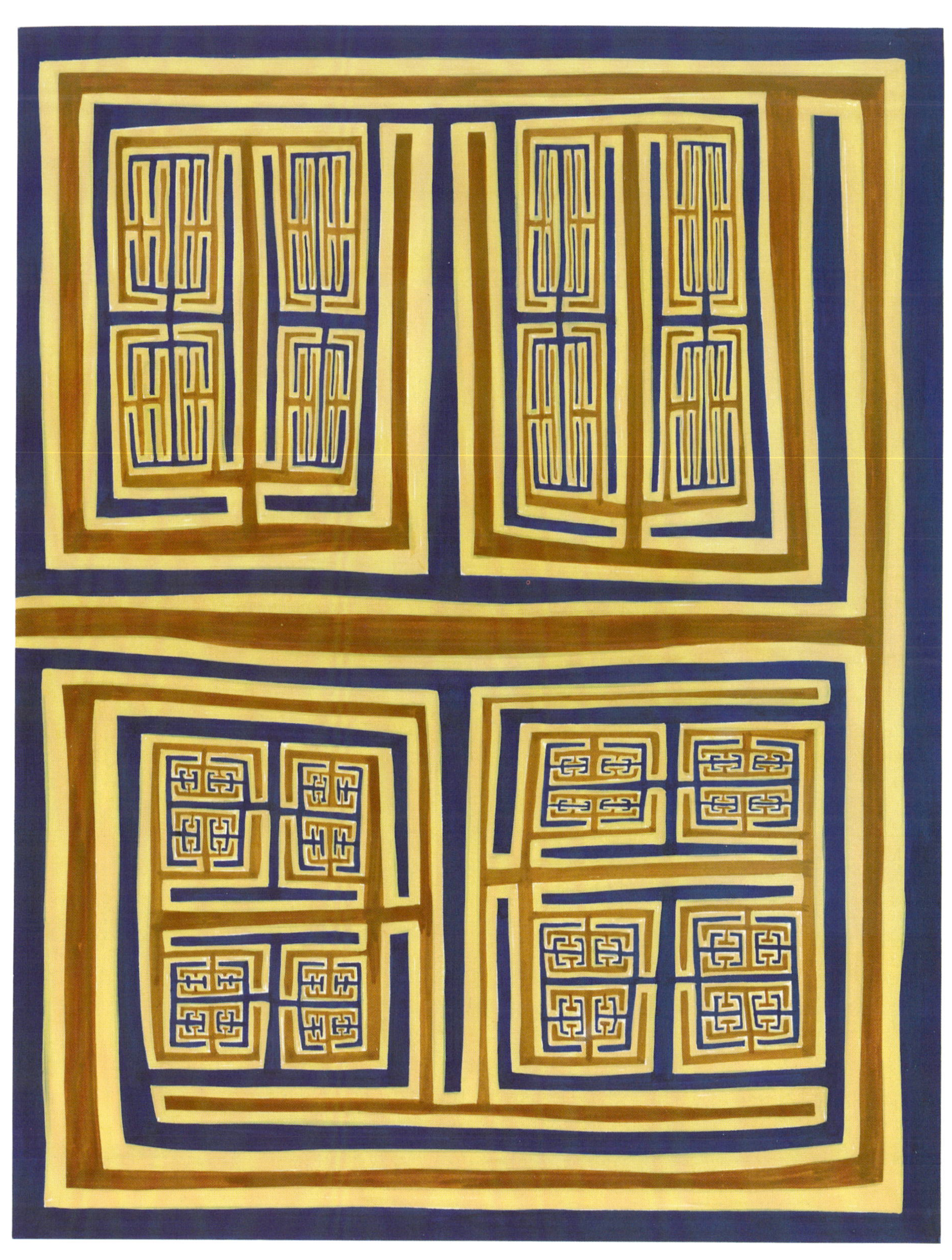

Multiply Recursive Combs (Second Version) 2005, gouache on paper, 11 1/2 x 9"

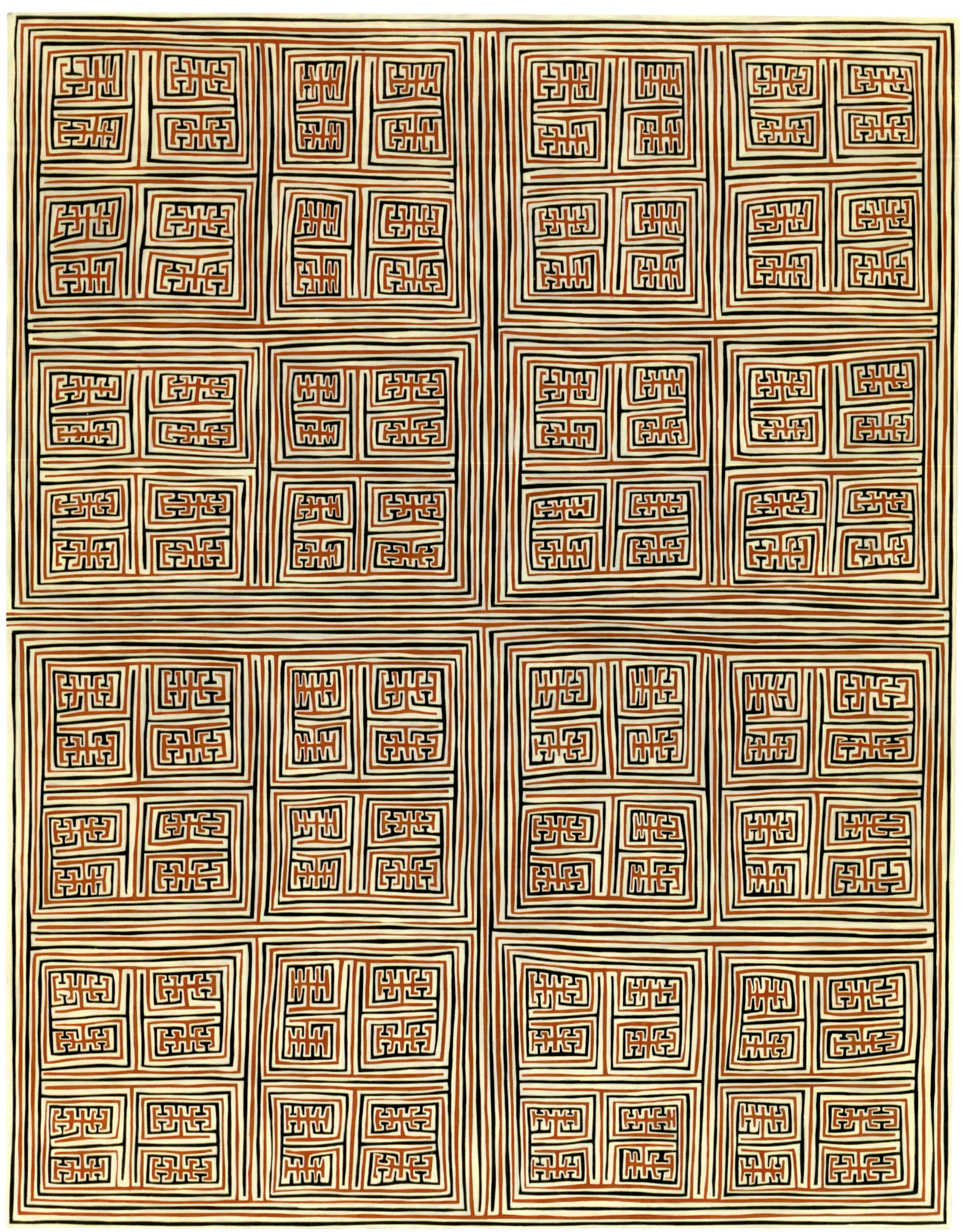

Multiply Recursive Combs 2005, enamel on aluminum, 19 1/4 x 15 1/8"

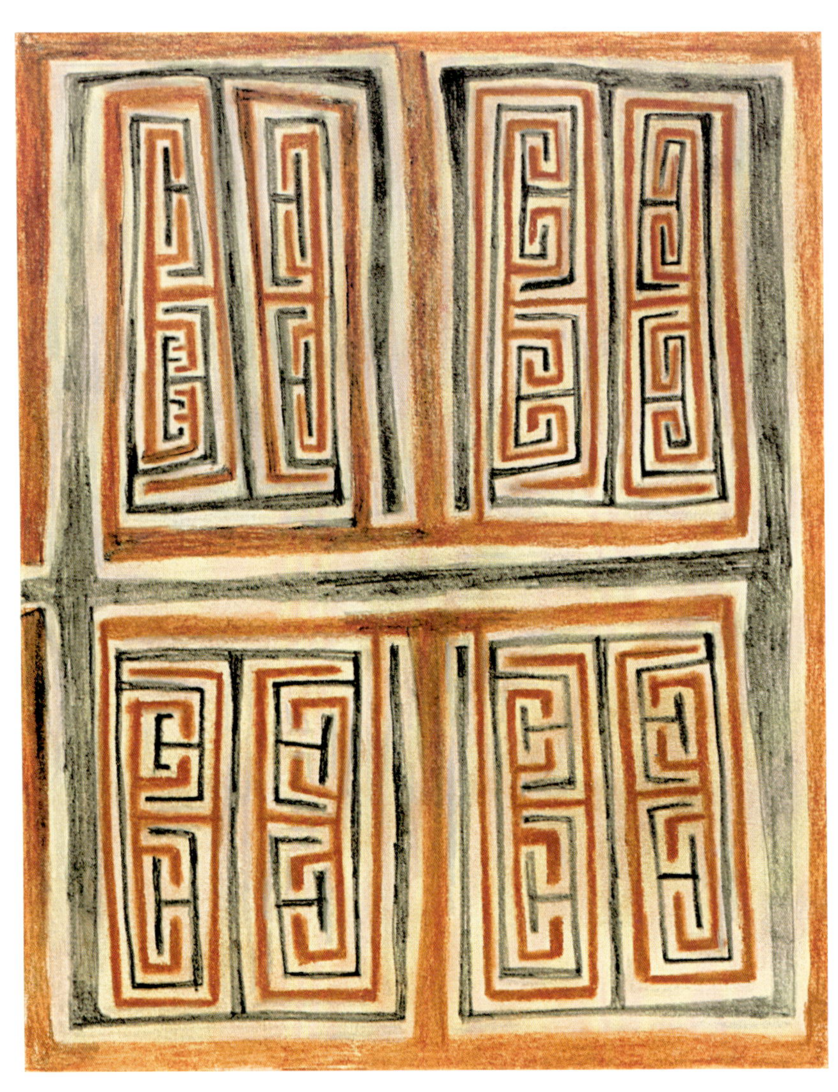

Multiply Recursive Combs 2005, conte and graphite on paper, 8 x 6 1/4"

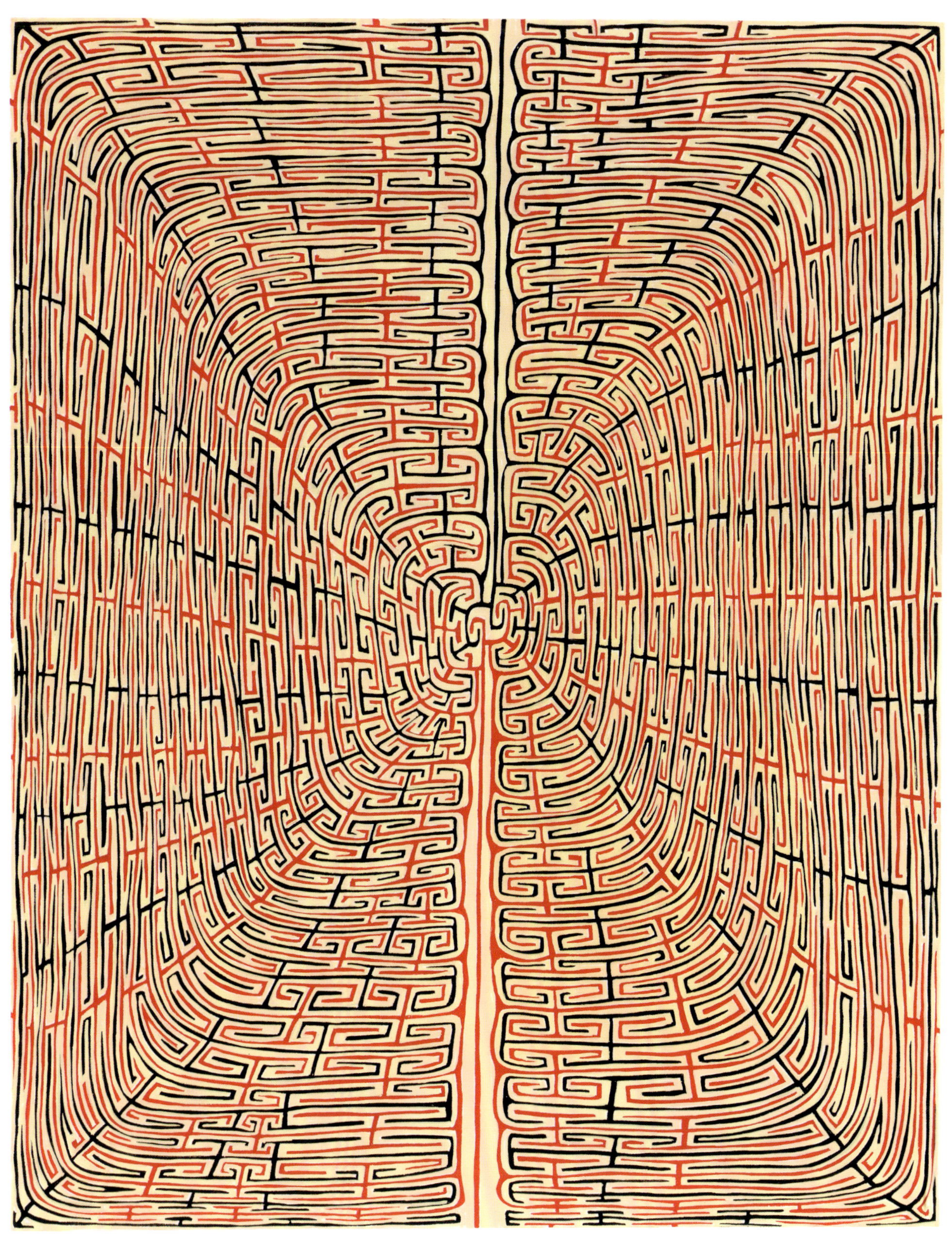

Two Forks, Red & Black   2005, gouache on board, 11 x 8 1/2"

Heliopolis 2005, enamel on aluminum, 29 x 22 3/4"

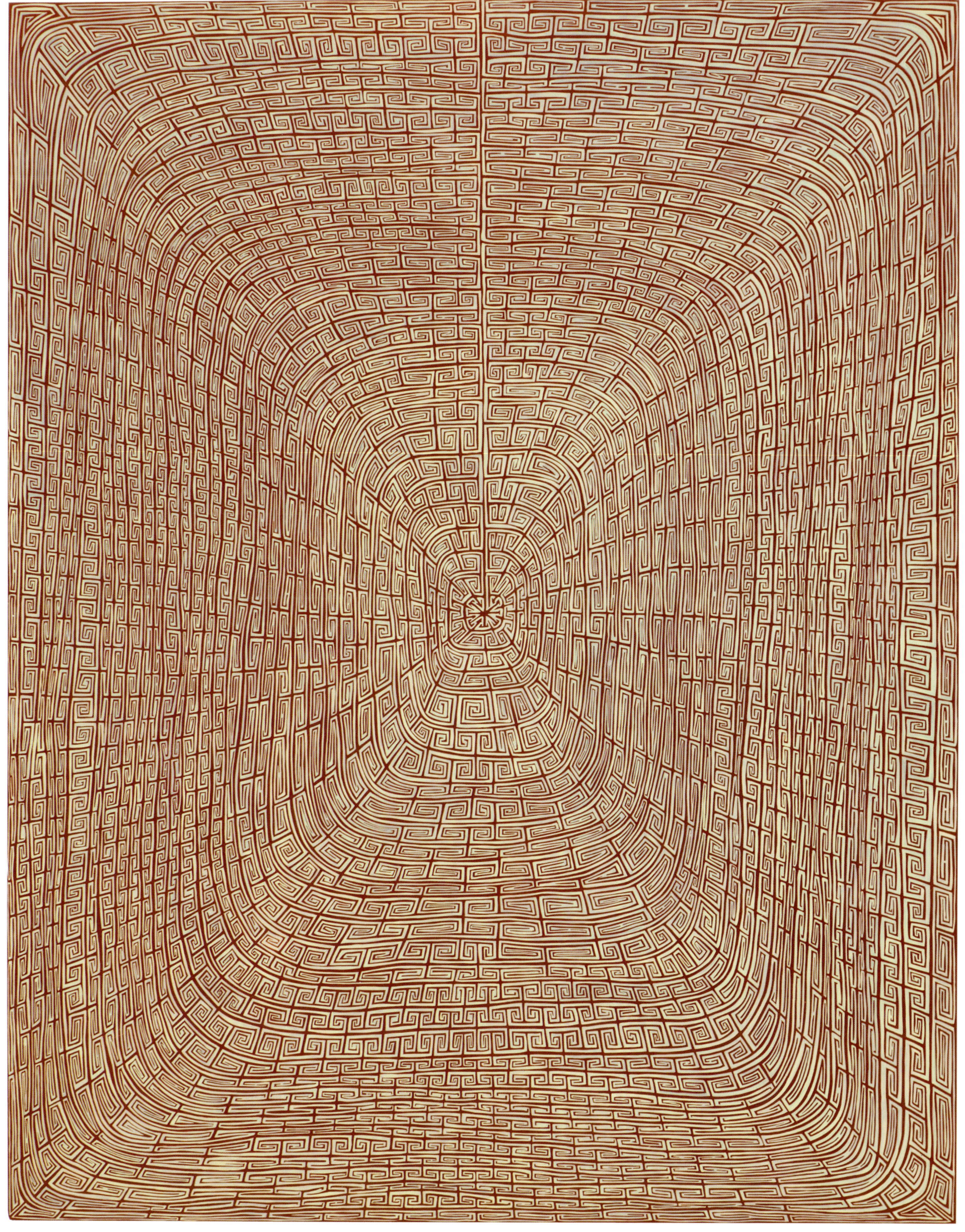

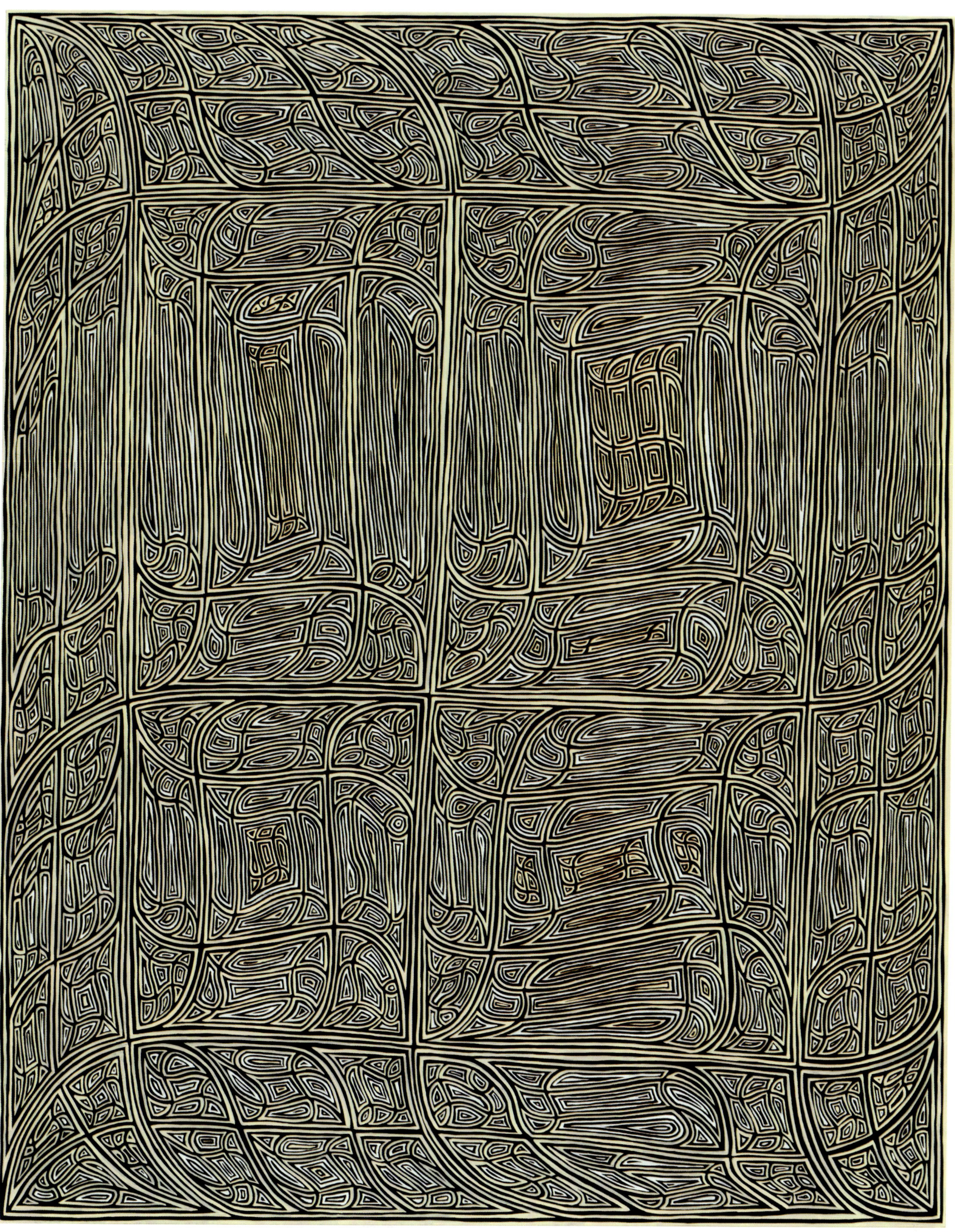

Recursive Lighthouse 2004, enamel on aluminum, 19 1/4 x 15 1/8"

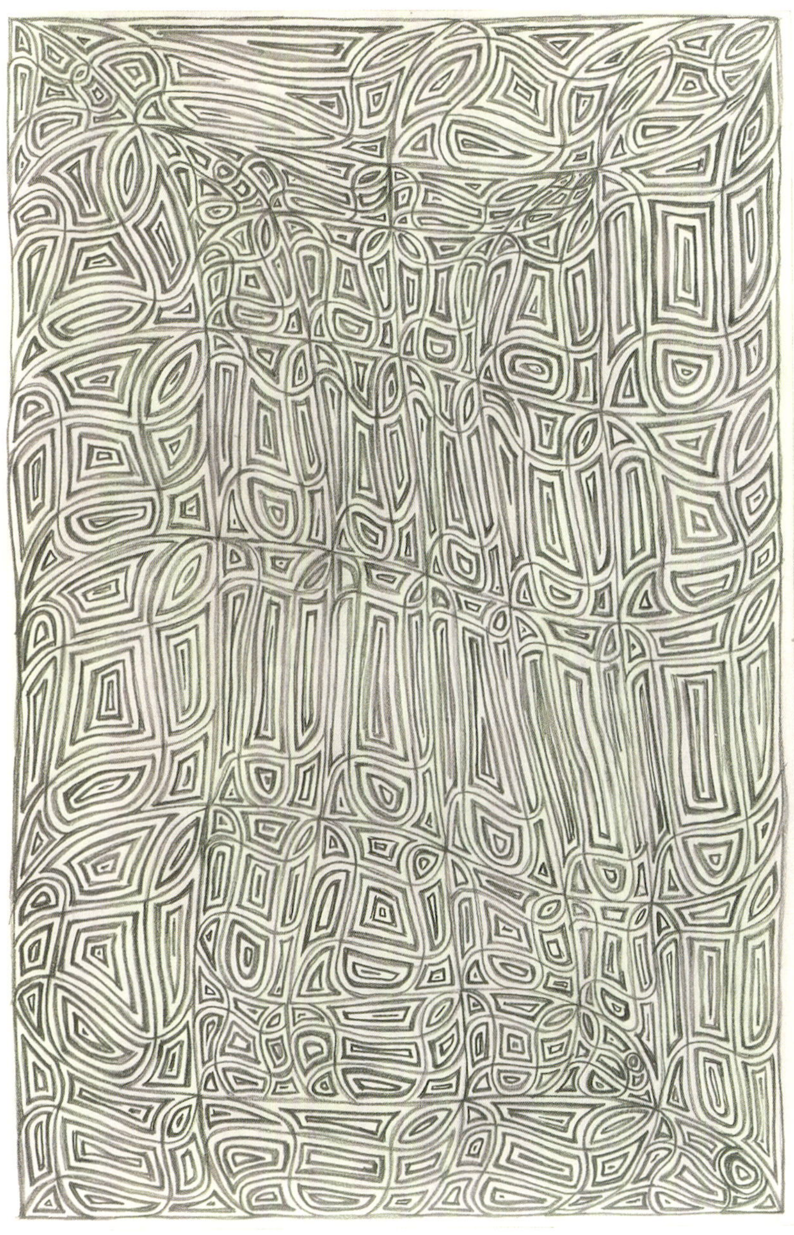

Recursive Lighthouse 2004, graphite on paper, 8 1/2 x 5 1/2"

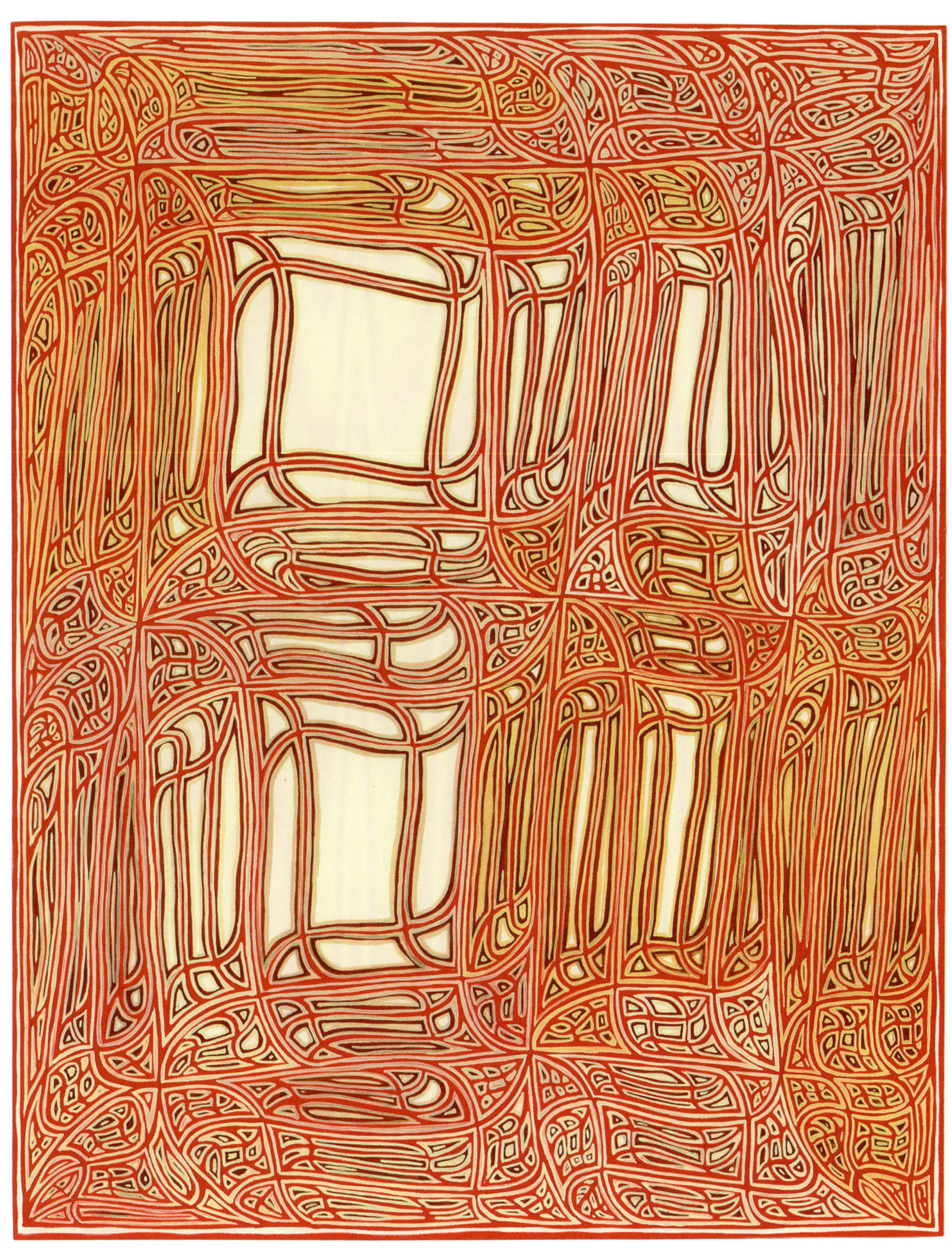

Recursive Lighthouse Variation 2004, gouache on paper, 11 1/2 x 8 7/8"

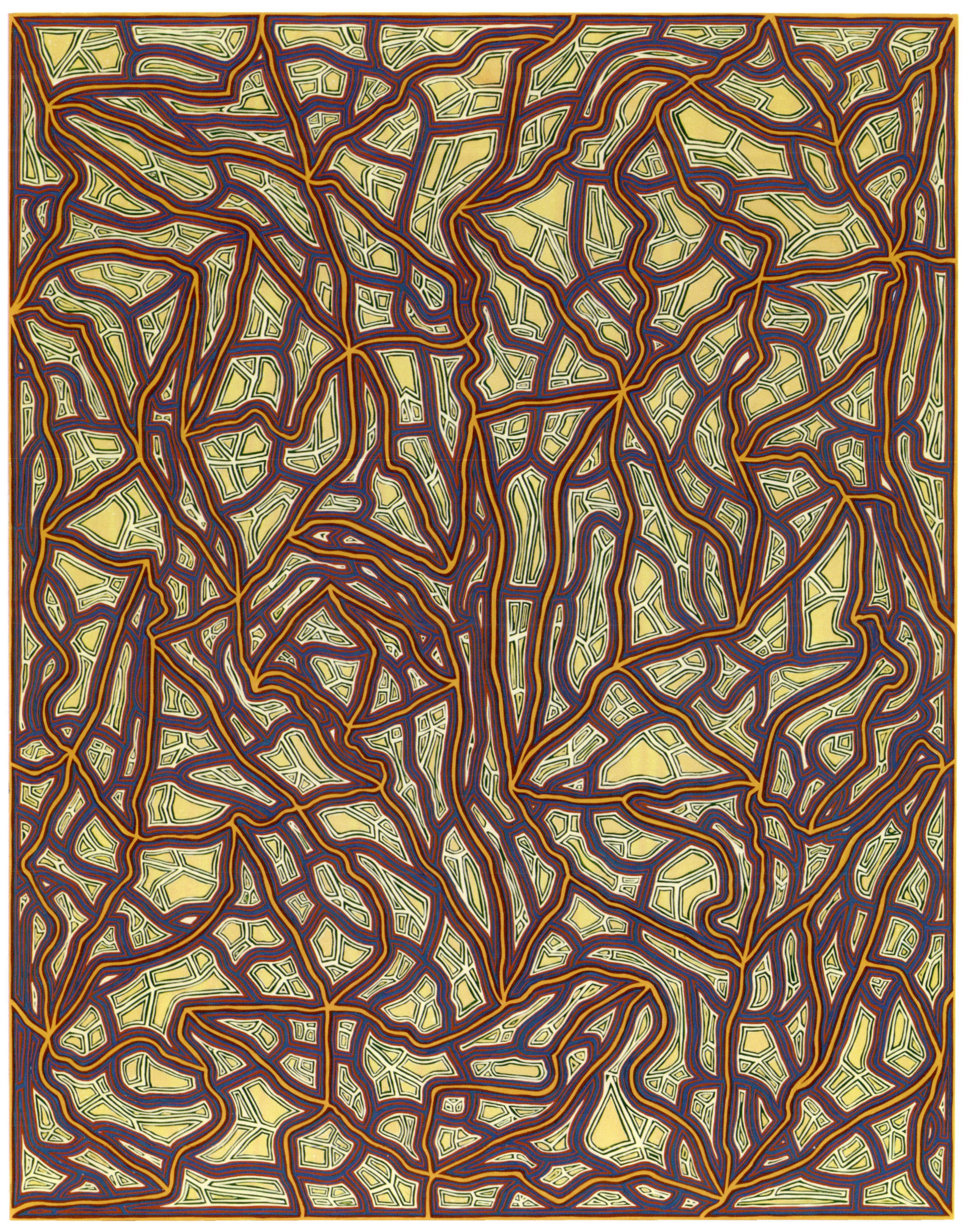

Distorted Overlapping Grids 2004–2005, enamel on aluminum, 19 x 15"

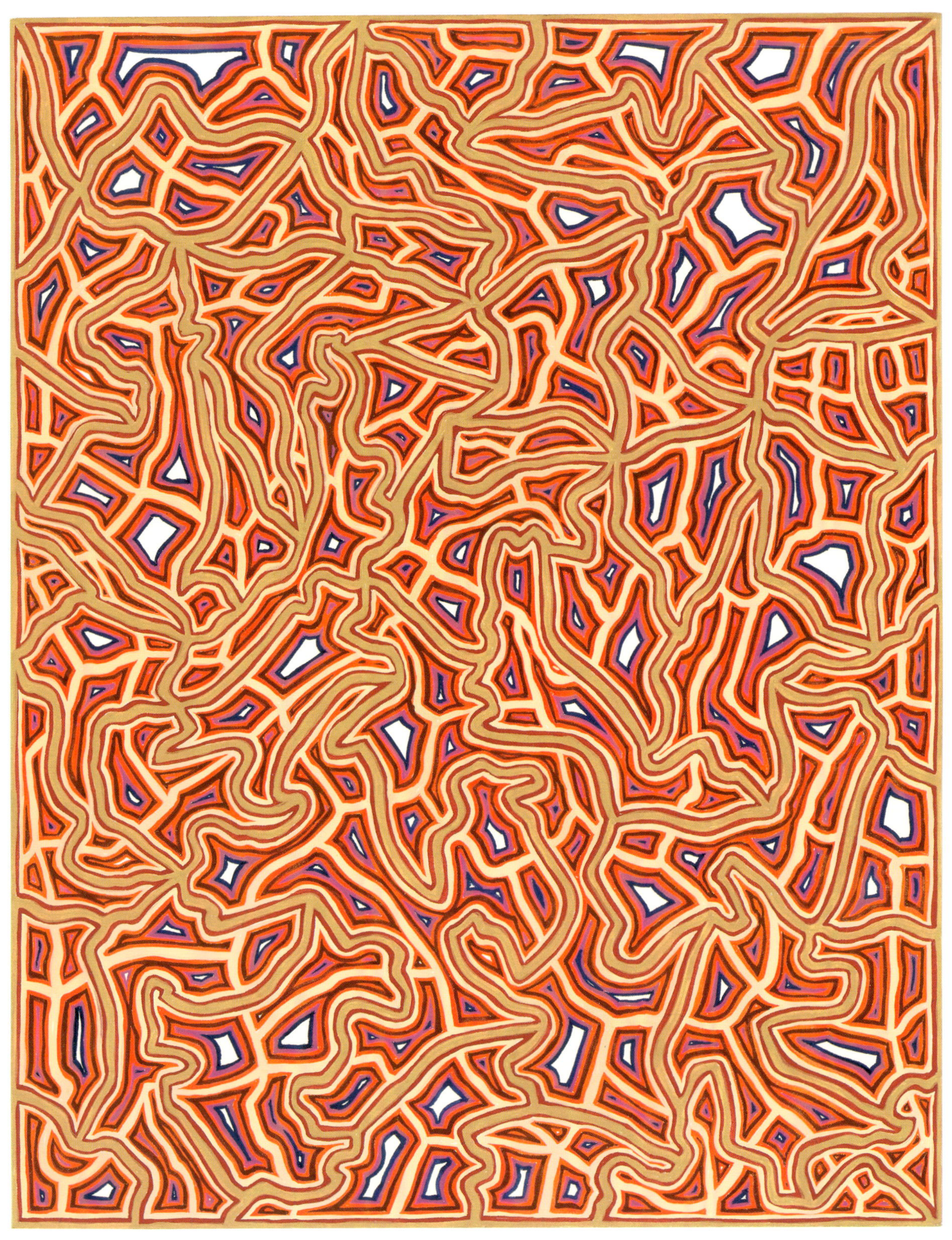

Distorted Overlapping Lattice 2004, gouache on paper, 11 x 8 1/2"

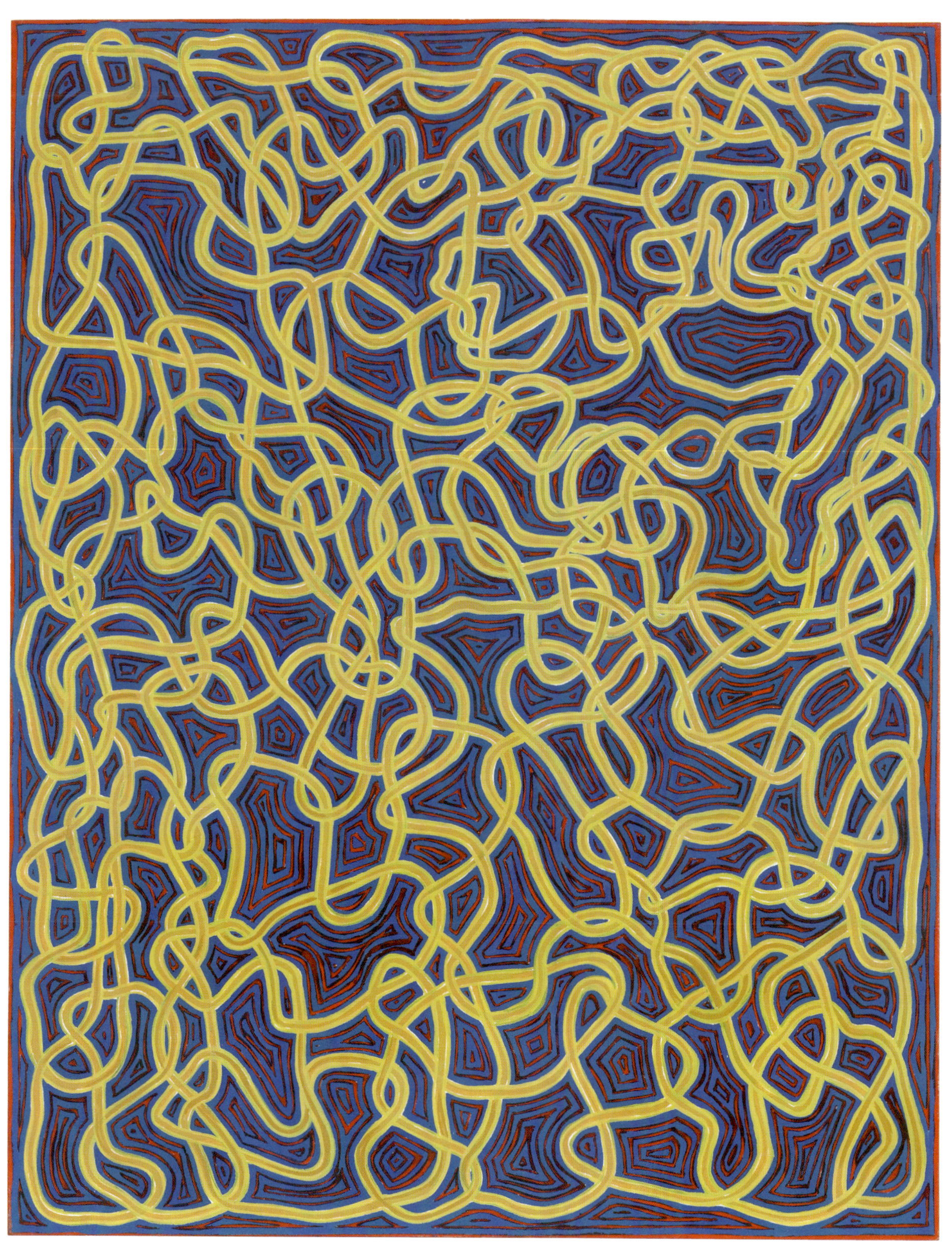

Unknot 2005, gouache on paper, 11 1/2 x 8 1/2"

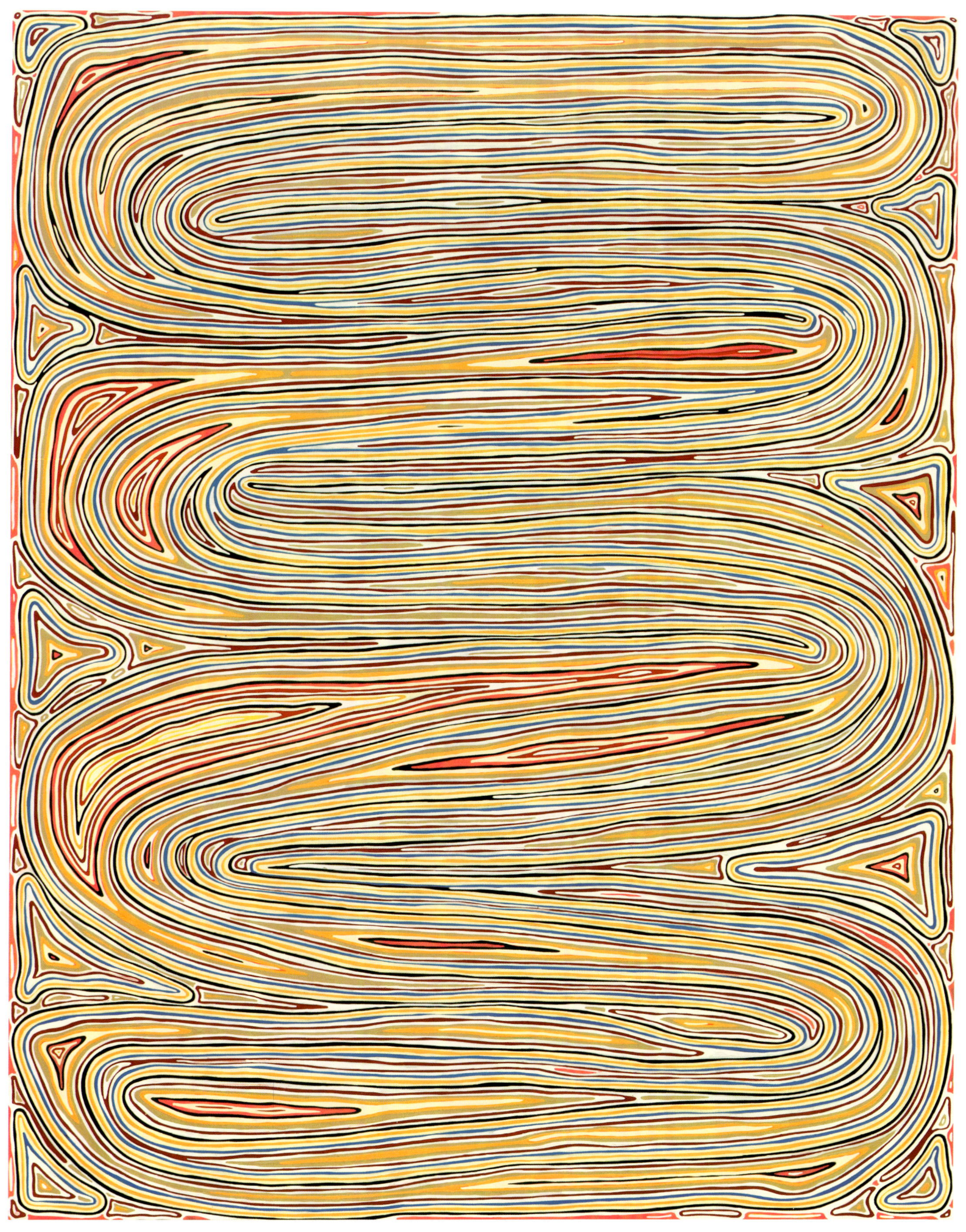

Nested Boustrophedonic Unknots 2004, enamel on aluminum, 19 1/4 x 15 1/8"

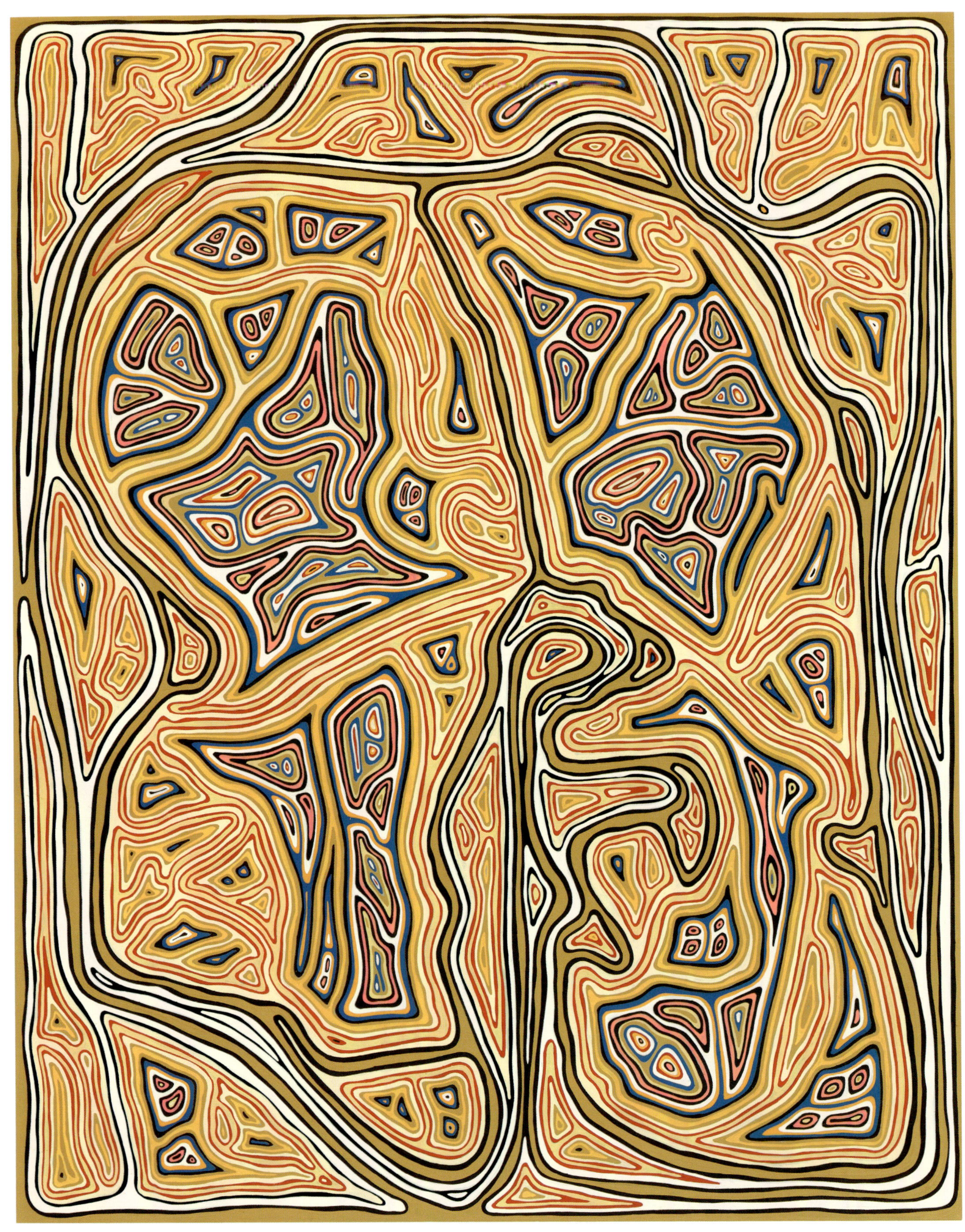

Non-Slice 2004, enamel on aluminum, 19 1/4 x 15 1/8"

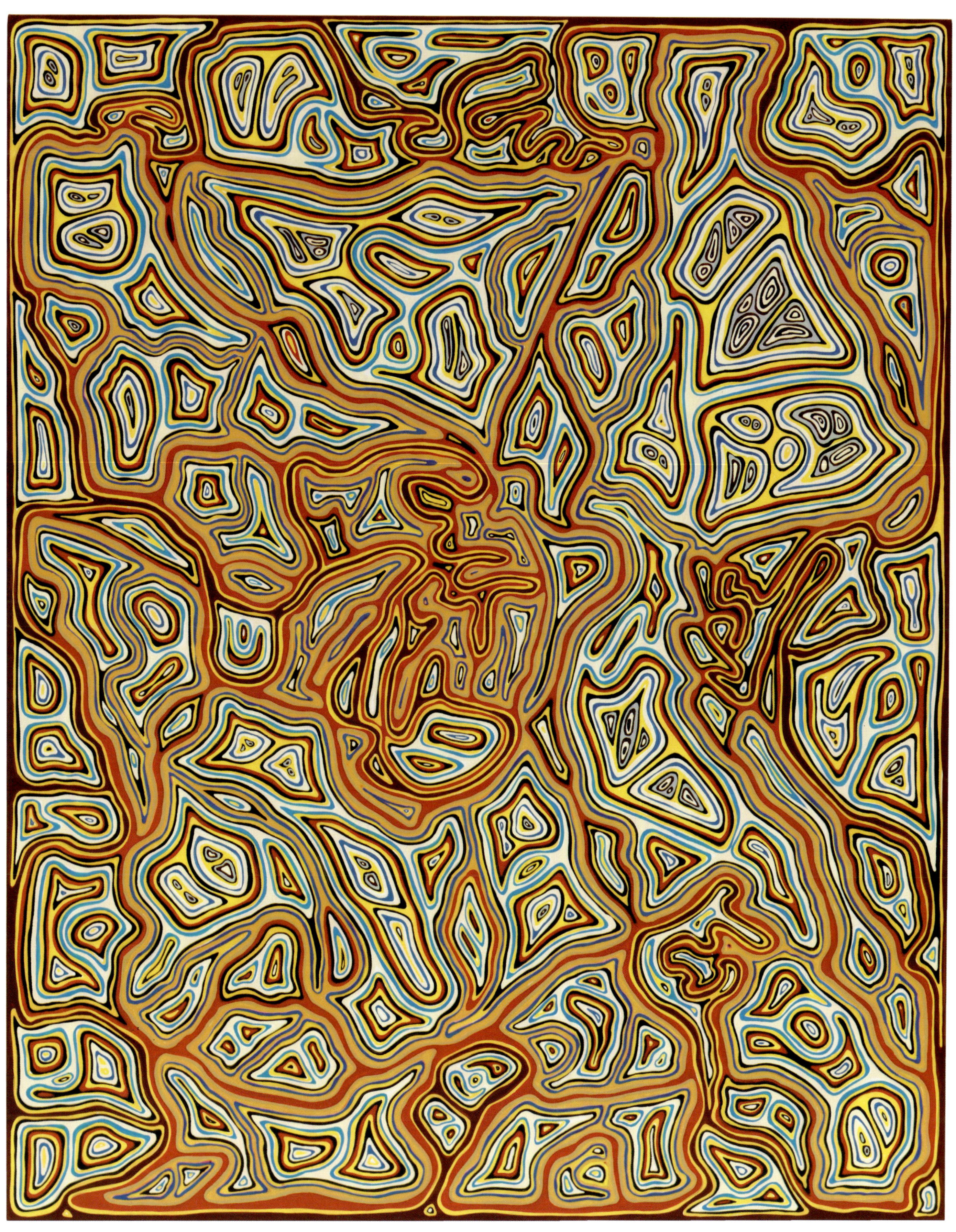

Non-Slice 2005, enamel on aluminum, 19 1/4 x 15 1/8"

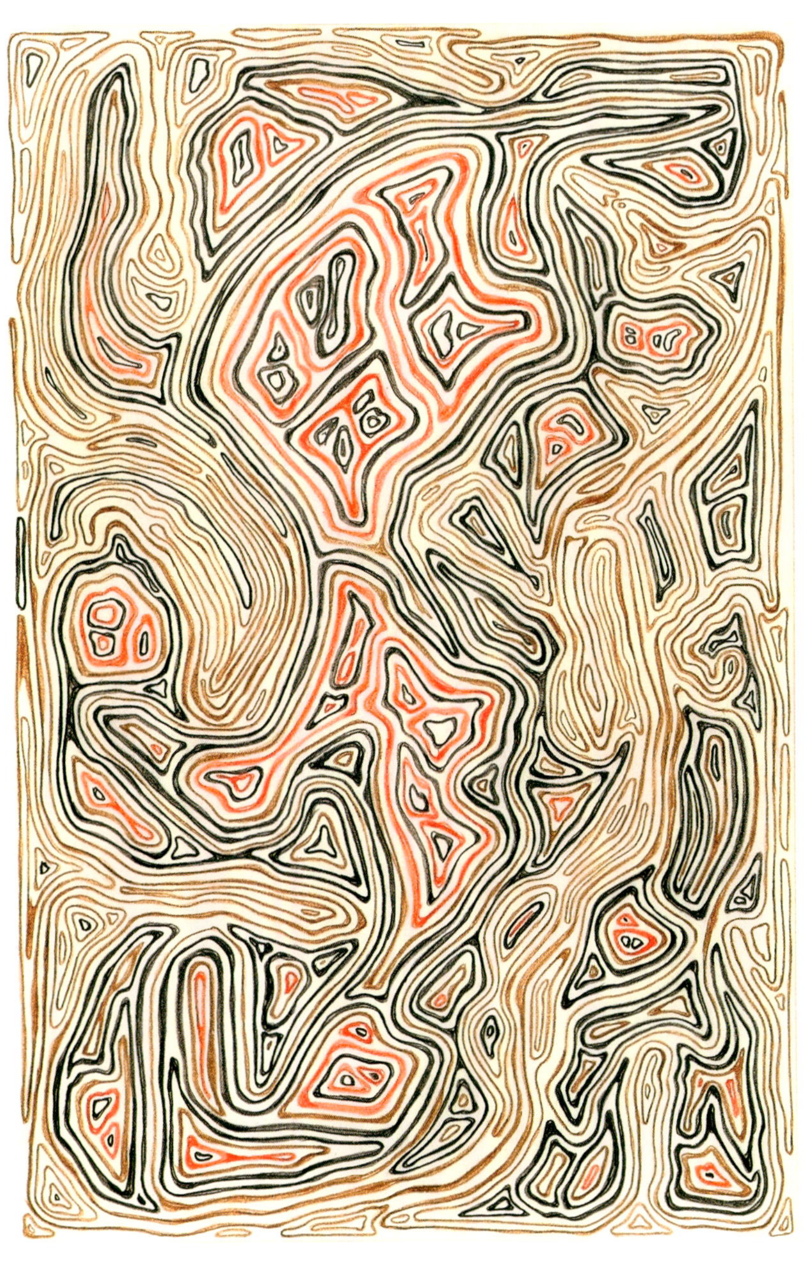

Slice 2004, graphite and colored pencil on paper, 8 1/2 x 5 1/2"

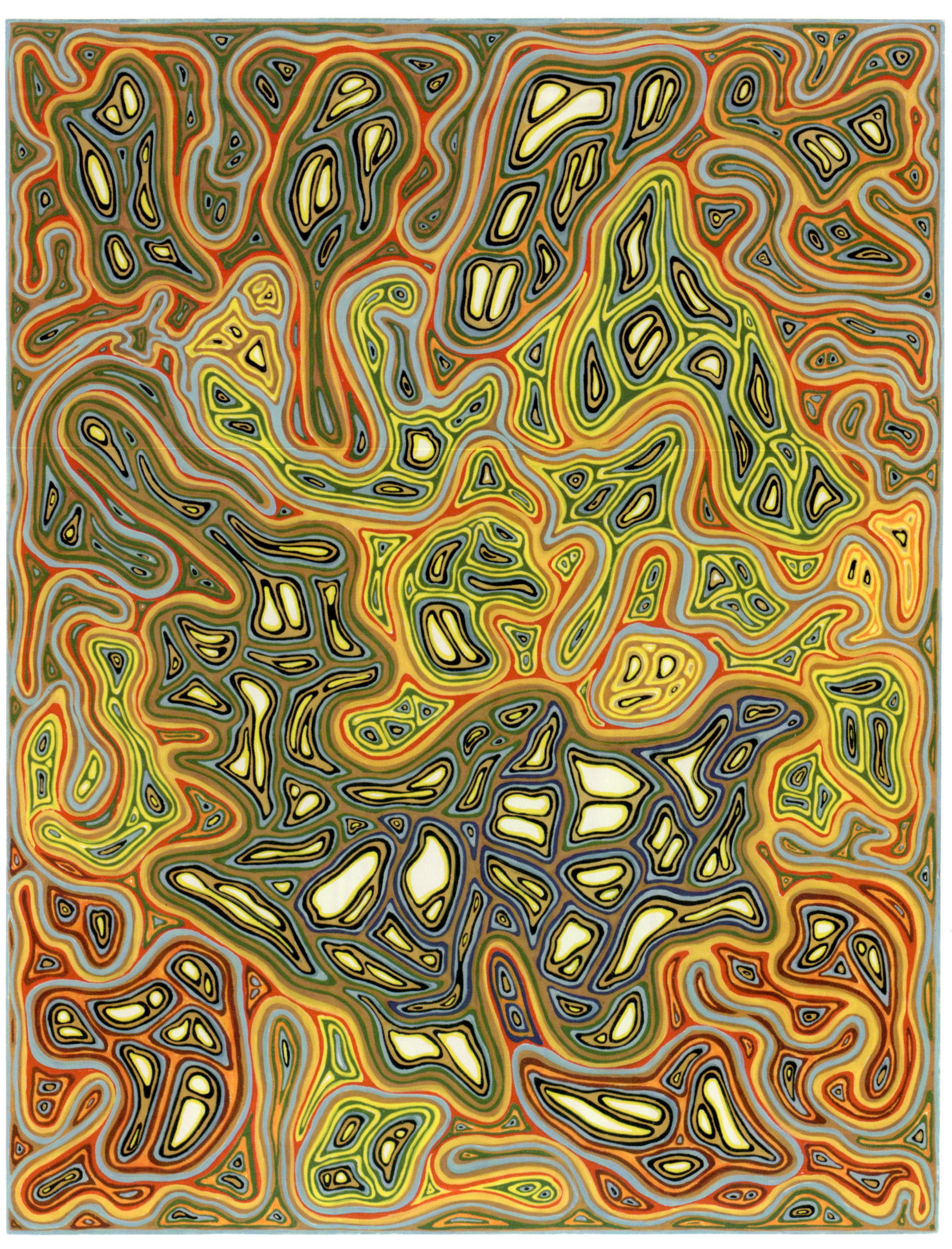

Acidic Non-Slice 2005, gouache on paper, 11 x 8 1/2"

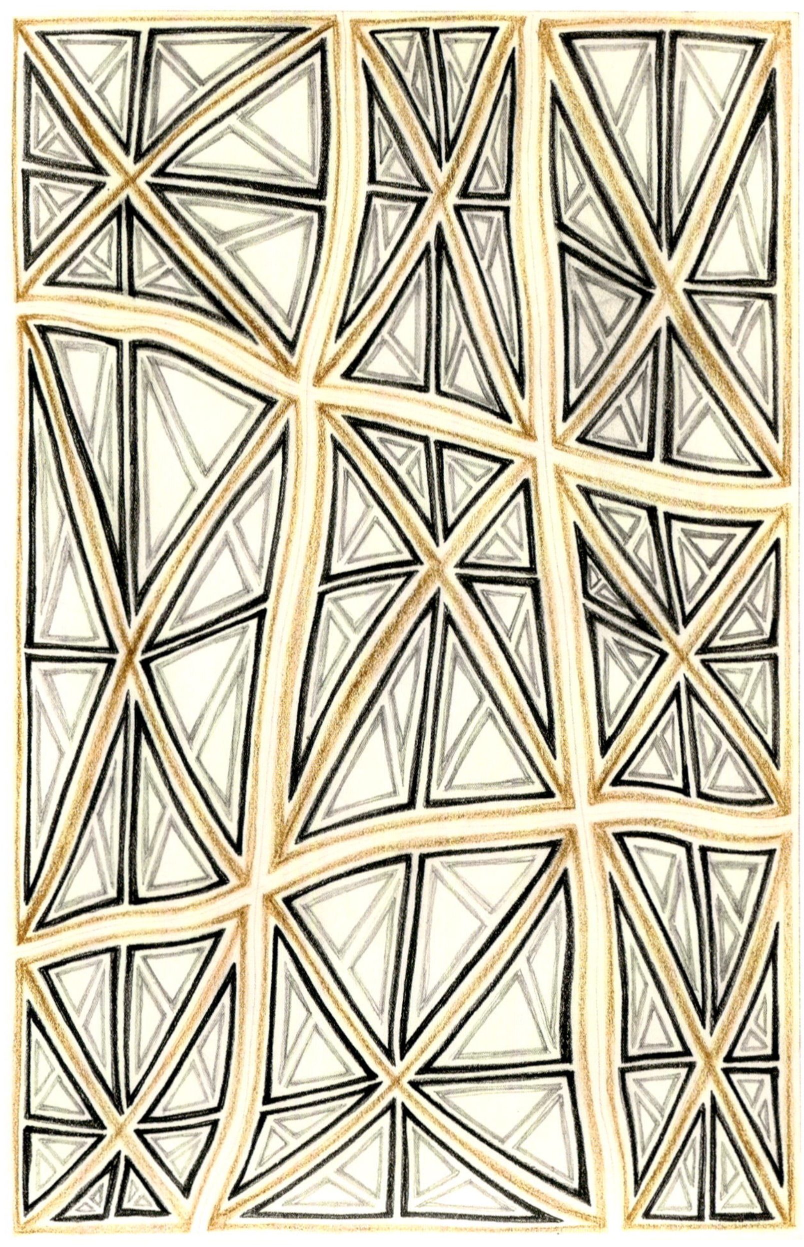

 Coffered Lattice (with Crosses) 2005, colored pencil and graphite on paper, 8 1/8 x 5 1/4"

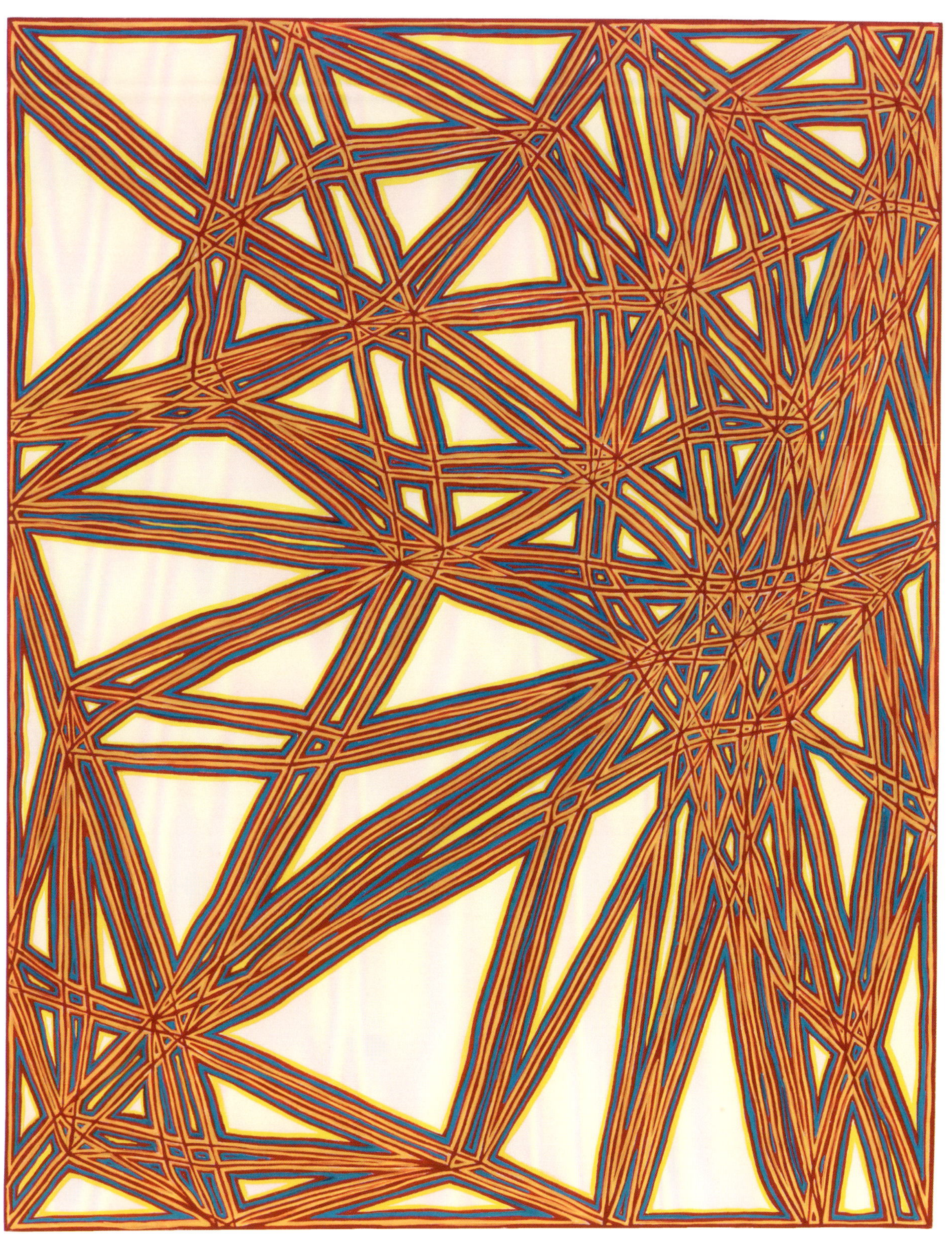

Shifted Lattice 2005, gouache on board, 11 x 8 1/2"

Shifted Lattice 2005, enamel on aluminum, 29 1/8 x 22 3/4"

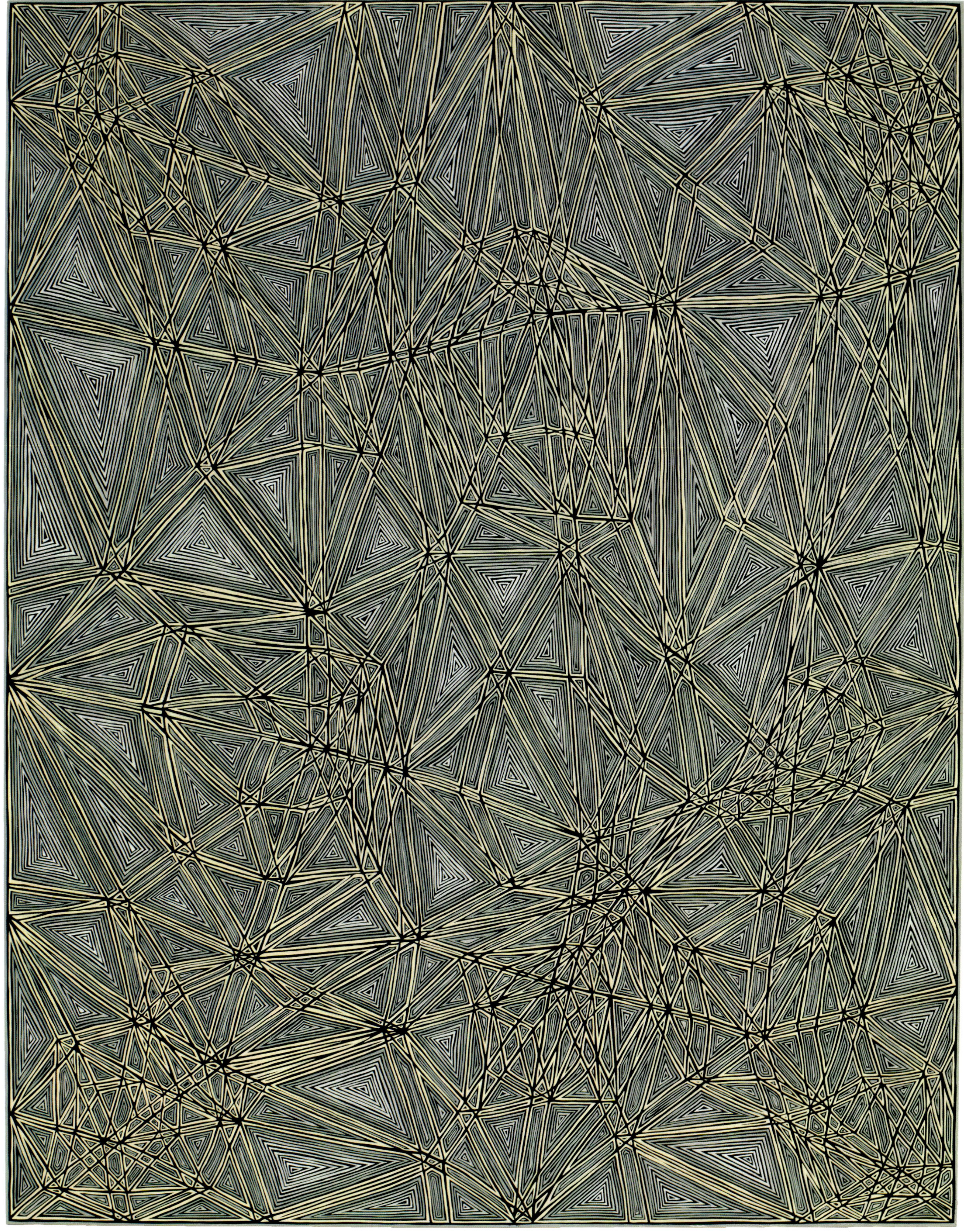

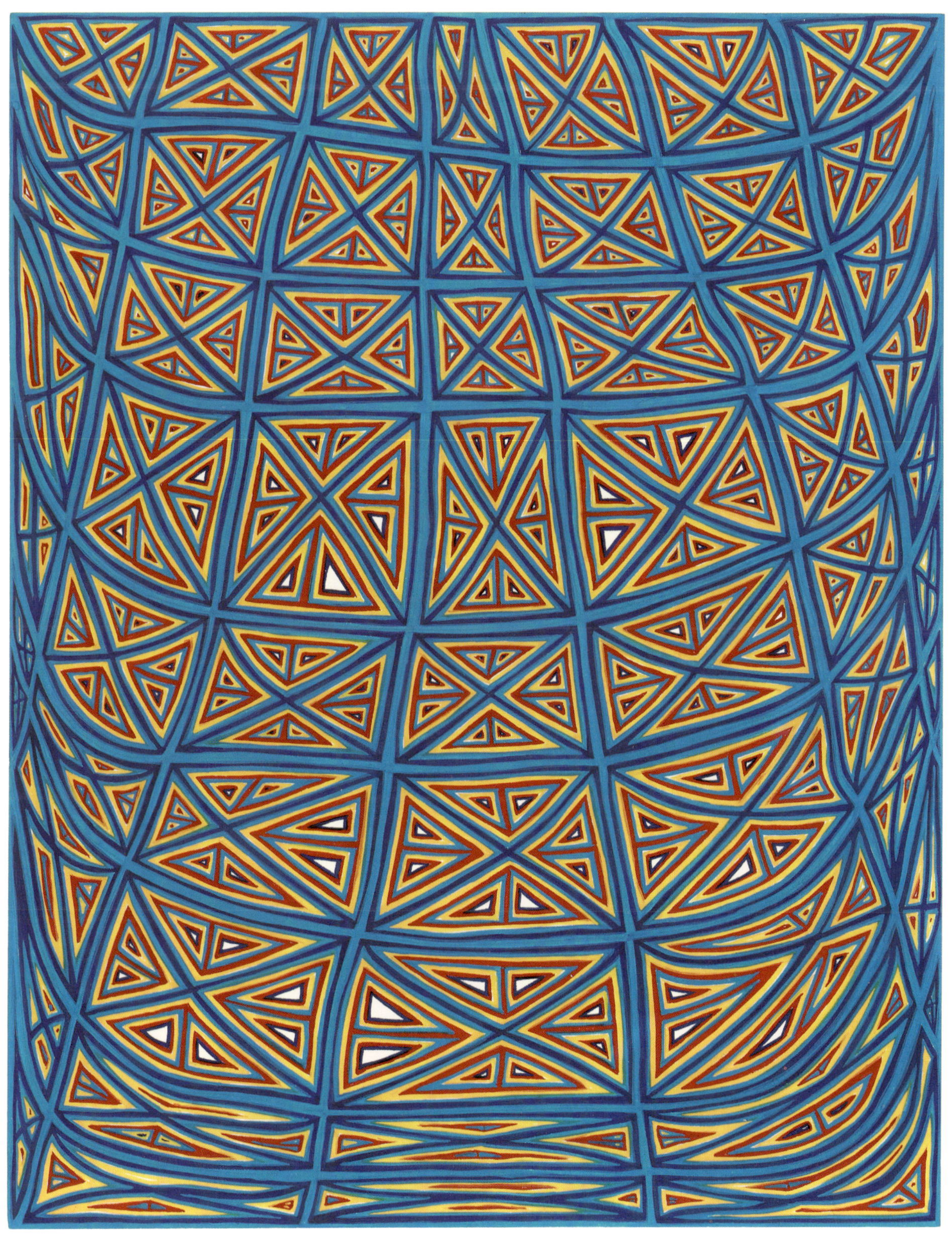

Sagging Grid 2005, gouache on paper, 11 x 8 1/2"

Coffered Divided Sagging Grid (with glitch) 2005, enamel of aluminum, 29 1/8 x 22 3/4"

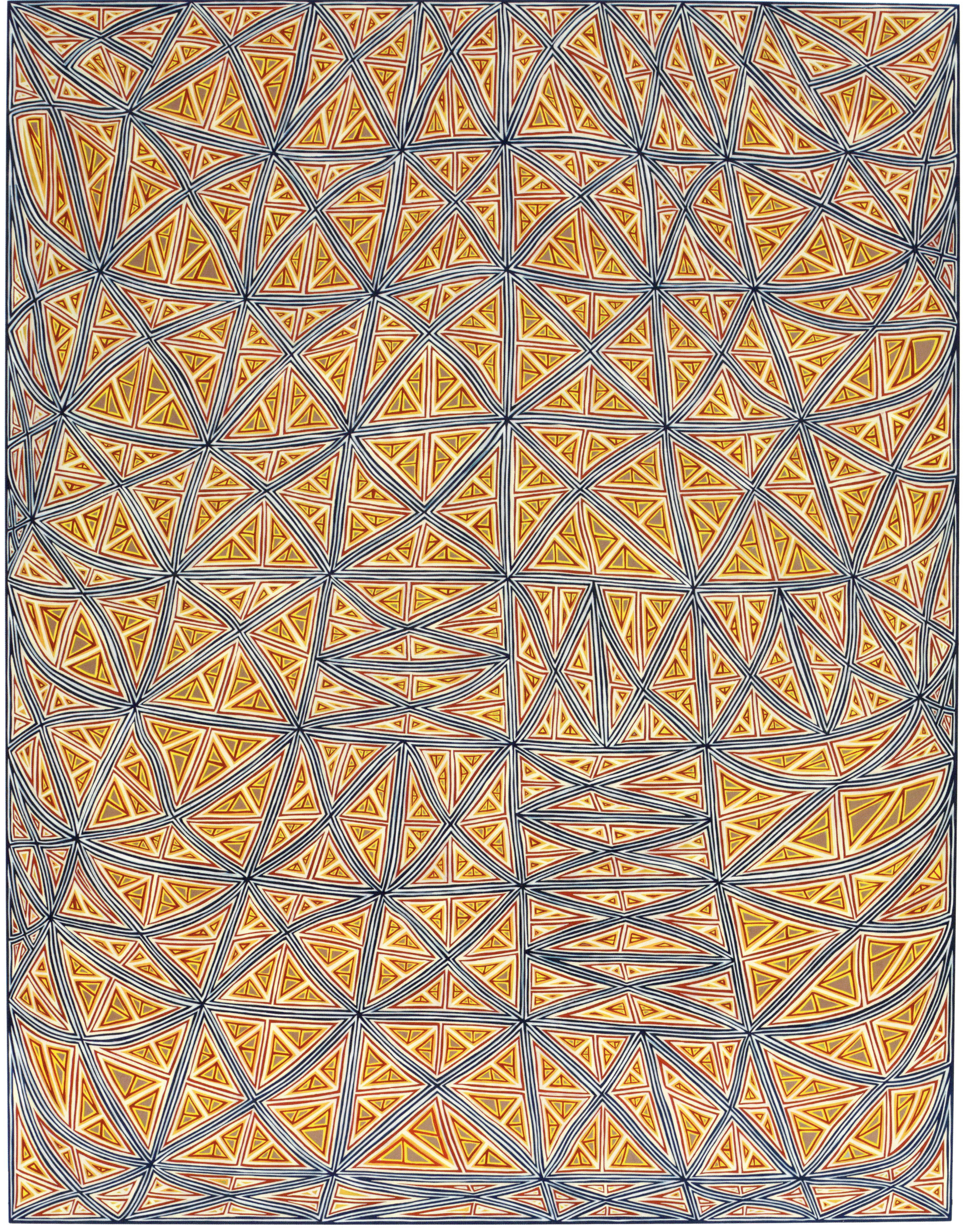

JAMES SIENA

BORN

1957 Oceanside, California
Lives and works in New York, NY

EDUCATION

1979 Cornell University, Ithaca, New York, B.F.A.

SELECTED SOLO EXHIBITIONS

1986 J. Noblett Gallery, Sonoma, California.

1996 Pierogi 2000, Brooklyn, New York.

1997–1998 Cristinerose Gallery, New York, November 20–January 10. (Catalogue; "The Finish Line," by Geoffrey Young)

1998 Daniel Weinberg Contemporary Art, San Francisco.

2000 Project Room, Gorney Bravin + Lee, New York, March 18–April 15.

Daniel Weinberg Gallery, Los Angeles.

2001 *1991–2001*, Gorney Bravin + Lee, New York, October 12–November 10.
(Catalogue; essay by Robert Hobbs, notes by James Siena)

2002 *Recent Paintings*, Daniel Weinberg Gallery, Los Angeles, April 27–May 8.

2003 Gorney Bravin + Lee, New York, June 6–July 31.

drawing and painting, San Francisco Art Institute/Walter Galleries, California, January 24–March 15.
Traveled to: The University of Akron, Ohio, March 31–April 25. (Brochure; text by Karen Moss)

2004 *Selected Paintings and Drawings 1990–2004*, Daniel Weinberg Gallery, Los Angeles, May 29–July 10.

2005 *Ten Years of Printmaking*, William Shearburn Gallery, St. Louis, Missouri, April 8–May 14.

Forthcoming: *New Paintings and Gouaches*, PaceWildenstein, 534 West 25th Street, November 18, 2005–January 28, 2006.

SELECTED GROUP EXHIBITIONS

1981 *By Other Means*, Just Above Midtown/Downtown, New York.

1987 *Atelier Conversations*, John Good Gallery, New York.

Jeffrey Neale Gallery, New York (three-artist exhibition with George Korsmit and Willy Heeks).

Wolff Gallery, New York.

J. Noblett Gallery, Sonoma, California (two-artist exhibition with Dan Schmidt).

1988 *Almost White*, Gabrielle Bryers Gallery, New York.

Wolff Gallery, New York (two-artist show with Cary Smith).

1989 *Drawings*, Wolff Gallery, New York.

The Art of the Computer and Xerox Machine, Minor Injury Gallery, Brooklyn.

1990 *A Question of Paint*, Hallwalls Contemporary Arts Center, Buffalo, New York.

1991 *The Painting Project*, Four Walls (organizer and participant), Brooklyn.

1992 *Vibology*, White Columns, New York.

1993 Nova Zembla, Hertogenbosch, The Netherlands.

Exquisite Corpse, Drawing Center, New York.

Group Grope, Geoffrey Young Gallery, Great Barrington, Massachusetts.

1994 Lipton Owens Company, New York.

Jobs Overseas, Kunstverein Munich.

Sworn Statements, Geoffrey Young Gallery, Great Barrington, Massachusetts.

The Beauty Show, Four Walls, Brooklyn.

1995 *Wheel of Fortune*, Lombard/Fried Fine Arts, New York.

Obsession, Chassie Post Gallery, New York.

Other Rooms, Ronald Feldman Gallery, New York, June 17–April 15.

Selections, Adam Baumgold Gallery, New York.

S. Cono Pizzeria, Brooklyn.

1996	*96 Works on Paper*, Geoffrey Young Gallery, Great Barrington, Massachusetts.
1997	*Tracery*, Betsy Senior Gallery, New York.
	All the Things You Are, Geoffrey Young Gallery, Great Barrington, Massachesetts.
1997–1998	*Current Undercurrent*, Brooklyn Museum of Art, New York, July 24–January 25.
1998	*Exploring Interior Landscape: Art from the Collection of Clifford Diver*, Delaware Art Museum, Wilmington, April 21–July 12. (Catalogue)
	The Risk of Existence, Phyllis Kind Gallery, New York.
	Wall Paper, Nicholas Davies Gallery, New York.
1999	*Free Coke*, Greene Naftali Gallery, New York, January 30–March 13.
	Rage for Art (Pierogi Reborn), Pierogi 2000, Brooklyn, February 12–March 15.
	Cyber Cypher Either Or, Mario Diacono Gallery, Boston.
	Trippy World, Baron/Boisante Gallery, New York.
	Invitational Exhibition, American Academy of Arts and Letters, New York.
	Pattern, Graham Gallery, New York.
	Ultra Buzz, Johnson County Community College, Overland Park, Kansas.
1999–2000	*New Work: Painting Today, Recent Acquisitions*, San Francisco Museum of Modern Art, California, December 17–March.
1999–2001	*post-hypnotic*, University Galleries, Normal, Illinois, January 12–February 21, 1999. Traveled to: McKinney Avenue Contemporary (MAC), Dallas, June 12–July 25, 1999; Contemporary Arts Center, Cincinnati, Ohio, September 4–November 7, 1999; Atlanta College of Art Gallery, Georgia, January 28–March 12, 2000; Chicago Cultural Center, Illinois, April 22–June 25, 2000; Tweed Museum of Art, University of Minnesota, Duluth, February 6–April 8, 2001. (Catalogue; essay by Barry Blinderman)
2000	*Greater New York*, P.S.1 Contemporary Art Center, Long Island City, New York, February 27–May.
	Invitational Exhibition, American Academy of Arts and Letters, New York, March 6–April 2.
	Fluid Flow, James Graham and Sons, New York, June 22–August 25.
	Mapping, Territory, Connexions, Galerie Anne de Villepoix, Paris, September 19–October 18.
2000–2001	*Art on Paper*, Weatherspoon Art Gallery, Greensboro, North Carolina, November 20, 2000–January 14.

2001	*By Hand: Pattern*, Precision, and Repetition in Contemporary Drawing, University Art Museum, California State University, Long Beach, August 28–October 14. (Catalogue)
	Accumulations, School of Art Gallery, Kent State University, Ohio, October 3–31.
	Repetition In Discourse, Painting Center, New York.
2002	*The Tipping Point*, Locks Gallery, Philadelphia, January 12–February 23. (Brochure; essay by David Cohen)
	New Editions, Senior and Shopmaker Gallery, New York, April–May.
	The 177th Annual: An Invitational Exhibition, National Academy of Design Museum, New York, May 1–June 9. (Catalogue)
	New Editions and Monoprints, Pace Prints, New York, June 19–July 12.
2002–2003	*The Fall Line*, OSP Gallery, Boston, December 3, 2002–January 25.
2003	*Black White*, Danese, New York, November 21–December 19.
2004	*Endless Love*, DC Moore Gallery, New York, January 7–February 7. (Brochure; text by Mark Greenwold)
	The 2004 Biennial, Whitney Museum of American Art, New York, March 11–May 31. (Catalogue; essays by Chrissie Iles, Shamim M. Momin, Debra Singer, et al)
	Summer 2004, PaceWildenstein, New York, July 8–September 10.
2005	*Sets, Series, and Suites: Contemporary Prints*, Museum of Fine Arts, Boston, January 19–May 30. (Catalogue)
	Super Cool, Kathryn Markel Fine Arts, New York, February.
	two d, Green On Red Gallery, Dublin, Ireland, February 17–March 12.
	Logical Conclusions: 40 Years of Rule-Based Art, PaceWildenstein, 534 West 25th Street, New York, February 18–March 26. (Catalogue; essay by Marc Glimcher)
	New acquisition installation, Johnson Gallery for Drawings and Prints, The Metropolitan Museum of Art, New York, April 26–July 24.
	Raising Questions: Contemporary Art from Madeline and Les Stern, Herbert F. Johnson Museum of Art, Cornell University, Ithaca, New York, May 21–July 30.
	Patterns and Grids, Pace Prints, New York, June 2–July 8.
	The 237th Royal Academy of Arts Summer Exhibition, London, June 7–August 15.
	Summer Group Show, PaceWildenstein, 534 West 25th Street, New York, July 14–August 25.

LIST OF WORKS

Cover:
one, one..., 2005 (detail)

Photography:
Aram Jibilian, pages 37, 49, 53
Ellen Labenski, pages 27, 29, 33, 41, 43, 47
Kerry Ryan McFate, pages 11–25, 28, 31, 34, 35, 38, 39, 42, 44, 45, 46, 51

Design:
Tomo Makiura

Production:
Paul Pollard
Tucker Capparell

Color Correction:
Motohiko Tokuta

Printing:
Meridian Printing, East Greenwich, Rhode Island

ISBN:
1930743548

Library of Congress Control Number:
2005909627